East Meets West

Diplomatic Gifts of Arms and Armour between Europe and Asia

Proceedings of the Royal Armouries conference
held at H. M. Tower of London
Saturday 14 September 2013

Edited by Thom Richardson

4 th
1613-2013
Four Hundredth
Anniversary
of Japan-British
Relations

First published in Great Britain in 2013 by
Royal Armouries, Armouries Drive,
Leeds LS10 1LT

© 2014 Royal Armouries

A CIP catalogue record for this book s available from the British Library

ISBN 978-0-948092-70-1

Contents

Preface

Thom Richardson
Keeper of Armour and Oriental Collections, Royal Armouries

2013 was an important anniversary for two of the objects in the Royal Armouries' collections, for it is 400 years since they were presented. The two armours, which form the focus of the first of the papers in this conference, were presented by the shōgun of Japan, Tokugawa Hidetada, to King James I of England through the agency of a captain of the East India Company, John Saris, whose mission was to travel to Japan with letters from King James and establish a trading agreement. One of the armours was put on display in the Tower Armouries by 1660, and remains to the present day a feature of the displays at the Tower. The commemoration of the 400th anniversary, Japan400, has included a wide variety of cultural events, some of them held at the Tower, including the presentation of a telescope (one of the gifts in 1613 to Tokugawa Ieyasu was a 'prospective glass' or telescope, mounted with silver gilt, thought to be the very first telescope to have left Europe) to Akira Matsura, the forty-first head of the Matsura family, former feudal lords of Hirado where Saris first landed in Japan.

In view of the significance of this anniversary of the museum's first Japanese acquisition it was thought appropriate to dedicate the museum's annual academic conference to the subject, through the theme of 'diplomatic gifts of arms and armour between Asia and Europe' (thanks to our former colleague Lynda Jackson for coming up with the racier title 'East Meets West'). The conference started with the main thematic study, on the Japanese gift armours. My colleague Ian Bottomley, now retired, did a good deal of important original research on the series of armours presented by Japan to the various states of Europe, and their provenances. He presented the latest state of his ongoing research to the conference.

Another colleague, Graeme Rimer, former Academic Director and Keeper of Firearms, has been engaged for many years in important research on one of the most iconic and controversial pieces of armour in England, the famous 'Horned Helmet' presented by Maximilian I to King Henry VIII. His original insight into the iconography of the piece forms the subject of the second paper. A third colleague, Guy Wilson, former Master of the Armouries, whose close collaboration with Moscow gave rise to the exchange of exhibitions between the Royal Armouries and the Moscow Kremlin back in the 1990s, next examines the exchanges of gifts between England and the courts of Russia and Spain in the 17th century.

The English were not the only nation active in Asia in the 17th century; the Dutch were there before them and the first Englishman in Japan, William Adams, arrived there as a pilot on a Dutch ship. Our colleague Eveline Sint Nicolaas of the Rijksmusem, Amsterdam, next presented her thoughts on two important groups of Asian arms in the collections of the Riksmuseum, the weapon cabinets of Cornelis Tromp and Michiel de Ruyter. Both these groups turn out to have fascinating provenances, which make the objects in them of far greater importance to the study of arms and armour than anyone expected.

The second half of the conference moved forward in time to the turn of the nineteenth century. One of the most distinctive groups of arms which were used as diplomatic gifts are the coral-mounted firearms of Algiers. The first ever study of this interesting group has been published by Niels Arthur Andersen of Copenhagen, whom I have had the pleasure of helping with his research for some 25 years. The book is called *Gold and Coral* and was published in 2014. We were privileged to have a preview of this work at the conference. This work is another example of how useful combining the study of physical objects and with the documentary history of their provenance can be. The role of these stunning objects in the complex diplomatic negotiations between the Deys of Algiers and the European powers that took place against the backdrop of the Napoleonic Wars can now be understood.

Provenance research also features in the next paper, a study by me and my colleague Natasha Bennett, into the story of the gift of arms and armour from India by the East India Company in 1853, one of the major founding gifts which established the Asian collection of the Royal Armouries. By painstaking research into the museum's convoluted records and forays into the archives of the East India Company we are able to reconstruct a glimpse of this story of collection building in the nineteenth century.

Another iconic piece from the Royal Armouries collection forms the subject of my colleague Nick Hall, Keeper of Artillery at our museum of artillery at Fort Nelson, near Portsmouth: the Dardenelles gun, one of the greatest surviving pieces of medieval Ottoman artillery. The story of how it came to be in Britain is told in his paper, which again uses archival research to rewrite a well-known story.

Soon after the gift of the Japanese armours to James I and the establishment of the East India Company's factory at Hirado, Japan was closed to foreign nations (except the Dutch), and centuries of isolation from the outside world followed. In the middle of the nineteenth century diplomatic relations were restored, and Japan underwent a great social, cultural and economic upheaval as it came to grips with the new order of the world. In the last paper in the conference my friend and colleague Greg Irvine, Senior Curator of Japanese art at the Victoria and Albert Museum, returns to Japan to examine the role arms and armour played in a new series of diplomatic gifts between East and West.

The Royal Armouries wishes to express its corporate gratitude, and I would like personally to extend thanks, to all the speakers and the efforts they have made individually and collectively to support the conference, especially to the Rijksmuseum for supporting Eveline's travel to the UK, to Japan400, co-ordinated by Nicolas Maclean and Tim Screech for their help in marketing the conference, to our Chairman Wes Paul, new Director General, Dr Edward Impey, and Head of Collections and Research, Suzanne Kitto, for supporting the conference, and to all the museum staff who have made it possible, especially Lynda Jackson, Carolyn Aldridge, Sabreena Craft, Chris Streek, Bridget Clifford and Kathleen McIlvenna, and to Debbie Wurr and Peter Armstrong for making this publication possible.

Japanese Diplomatic Gifts of Arms and Armour to Europe
of the Sixteenth and Seventeenth Centuries

Ian Bottomley
Curator Emeritus, Royal Armouries

This paper represents a synthesis of my research into this topic, some of which has been published previously. New evidence has come to light that has necessitated the revision of some of earlier findings and the re-evaluation of others. There are still unpublished documents known to exist that could change the picture further one day.

Towards the end of the fifteenth century the two great seafaring nations, Spain and Portugal, were in dispute over who should have claim to any lands yet to be discovered. Various popes made attempts to settle matters by allocating different areas of the globe to the two countries, but with little lasting success. Ultimately it was recognized that the only satisfactory solution lay in dividing the world into hemispheres; this was formalized in the Treaty of Tordesillas of 1494, in which a meridian some 100 leagues west of the Azores and Cape Verde islands was chosen as the dividing line. Spain's region of influence was to lie to the west, while Portugal was allocated all the lands to the east of the line. After mapping the coast of Africa and establishing a base at Goa in India in 1510, the Portuguese sailed further east to China and finally reached Japan in 1543. This momentous event occurred when a storm forced a Chinese ship with three Portuguese merchant adventurers on board to take shelter at the island of Tanegashima, just off the southern tip of Kyushū. Who exactly these pioneers were remains a matter of dispute, but one was almost certainly Christopher da Molta, being named in Japanese texts as Kirishitamota.[1] This accidental visit was to

---

1   R. Daehnardt, *Espingarda Feiticeira* (Lisbon, 1994), 6ff.

have a profound effect on Japanese history. Not only did it open the way for trade between the two countries and the conversion of many Japanese to Catholicism, but also the guns the Portuguese carried were in due course to determine Japan's political destiny.

On their arrival the Portuguese found Japan in the throes of sporadic but widespread civil wars. So devastating were these conflicts that this period, lasting approximately 170 years, is now known as the *Sengoku Jidai* or 'Age of the Country at War'. It was an era that had seen one territorial lord after another gain some local supremacy only to be defeated and toppled, none being able to build a sufficiently large power-base from which to launch an attempt to unify the country. It was the more forward-thinking of these lords, the *daimyō*, who recognized the gun's potential and realized that these weapons could break the stalemate of the wars.

The central Japanese authorities, preoccupied with the country's internal problems, paid little attention to the newly arrived Europeans other than granting them permission to trade and preach their faith. Following in the wake of the traders were Jesuit priests who controlled Portugal's Far Eastern operations. It was these priests who grasped the opportunity for a lucrative import and export business between Japan and China. Diplomatic relations between these two countries had been strained for some time and the Japanese were having difficulty in satisfying their demand for Chinese brocades and raw silk. Such trade as did exist was largely in the hands of merchant sailors, who were in most cases little more than pirates. It was the depredations of these *wako* on the coastal settlements of China that was the reason for the animosity between the two countries. Using their Indian and Chinese bases the Jesuits established a three-legged trading route. Each journey involved shipping goods from Goa to Macao where they were exchanged for items in demand in Japan. These goods were then landed at ports such as Yamagawa, Usuki, Hirado and later Nagasaki, where they were exchanged for commodities such as copper, ceramics and lacquer ware for the return voyage to India and ultimately Europe. Each round trip was so profitable that it was reckoned to double the initial outlay.

It was natural that the daimyō of Kyūshū should vie with each other to have the Portuguese 'Black Ships' unload these very desirable and profitable commodities at their ports. Ōtomo Yoshishige, daimyō of Bungo province (1530–87), aware that a diplomatic gesture might gain him an advantage over his rivals, sent the young king of Portugal, Sebastian (1557–78), a *tantō* or dagger decorated with a gold snake wrapped around the scabbard in 1562. Unfortunately the gift never reached its intended recipient, being damaged in a storm and having to be returned to Japan for repair.[2] He also sent the Portuguese viceroy of Goa, Antão de Noronha, a gift that included an armour and two silver mounted *naginata,* that were said to have been very favourably received.[3] In the same year Yoshishige became a Buddhist monk taking the name Sanbisai Sōrin, a conversion that did little to curb his military ambitions. In 1578 he converted to Christianity to ingratiate himself yet further with the Portuguese, taking the name Francisco on his baptism. He died at the battle of Mimigawa fighting the Shimazu family of Satsuma province.

These early decades of Portugal's involvement in Japan, dominated as they were by trade and religious conversions, were not to last. The political situation in Portugal had become unstable when Sebastian died without heir. His uncle, Cardinal Henry (1557–80) succeeded him but died only two years after his accession. While the Portuguese were casting around for yet another suitable candidate to take the throne, King Philip II of Spain (1527–98) seized the moment and marched into Lisbon, becoming the ruler of the whole Iberian peninsula. For the Jesuits in the Far East this was worrying news. The unification of the two countries had, in effect, negated the treaties that had given Portugal the sole rights to trade and gain converts in the East. For thirty years the Jesuits had managed to retain control of the region's trade with Europe and, just as importantly to them, had kept the Spanish, and in particular the monks of the Franciscan order, out of the area. With a Spanish king now on the throne of Portugal there was the very real fear that Philip would break the Jesuit monopoly.

After due consideration it was decided that a scheme was needed to persuade the fiercely Catholic Philip of the splendid progress being made in converting the Japanese to the Catholic faith. In 1582 Father Alessandro Valignano (1539–1606) persuaded three Kyushū daimyō, Ōmura, Ōtomo and Arima, to assist in financing a mission to send

2   C. R. Boxer, *The Christian Century in Japan 1549–1650* (Berkley, 1951), 96.
3   Ibid.

a group of Japanese Christians to the Spanish court. As a secondary benefit it was believed that these converts would be so awed by the splendours of European architecture, culture and learning that on their return they would spread word throughout Japan of the advantage of converting to Christianity. Ultimately four baptized Japanese youths were selected to sail to Spain and Italy by way of Africa with Father Valignano and Father Diogo Mesquita, their tutor. The four Japanese, all baptized Christians, were Mancio Ito, their spokesman, Miguel Chijiwa, Julião Nakaura and Martinão Hara.[4]

This momentous journey, known in Japan as the Tenshō mission after the year period in which it sailed, was seen by other daimyō as a way of strengthening the diplomatic ties between Japan and Europe. Oda Nobunaga (1534–82), one of the leading daimyō of the era, and his vassal, Hashiba Hideyoshi (1537–98), sent gifts to the Jesuits on Kyushū to be given to European dignitaries. Hideyoshi had been born a peasant, but had risen to power as one of Nobunaga's senior generals by reason of his exceptional military ability. He is better known by the name granted to him later, Toyotomi Hideyoshi. Nobunaga, who had conquered a considerable part of Honshu, was heavily involved in fighting while preparations for the mission were being put in place. He was known to be friendly towards the foreigners and fascinated by their culture, so it is understandable that he should take this opportunity to ingratiate himself further by contributing gifts. Hideyoshi on the other hand was less sympathetic towards the Portuguese. Following the unification of Japan and his elevation to the position of regent, he issued an edict proscribing Christianity, but failed to enforce it with any vigour. It seems strange therefore that he felt obliged to donate expensive gifts to the venture unless his motive was to gain favour with his lord.

During the same year that the mission was being organized, Nobunaga had dispatched his generals to attack various castles and strongholds on Honshu occupied by some of the few daimyō that still opposed him. Confident that matters were in capable hands, he took the opportunity to travel to Kyoto to rest. Hideyoshi was given the task of subduing Takamatsu Castle in Bitchu province, held by the Mori

---

4   N. Watanabe (ed.), *The World and Japan: Tensho and Keicho Missions to Europe 16th–17th Centuries* (Sendai, 1995), catalogue no. 72.

clan of Nagato province. Another of Nobunaga's trusted generals, Akechi Mitsuhide (1528–82), was ordered to join Hideyoshi and aid him in the assault but for reasons that have never been satisfactorily explained Akechi disobeyed the order and instead marched on Kyoto. The greater number of his troops was ordered to attack Nijo Castle while Akechi and a smaller forced moved on Honno-ji, the temple in which Oda was staying. Taken completely by surprise and totally outnumbered, Oda committed suicide and ordered the temple to be burned to stop his head being taken. Akechi sought out one of Oda's sons, Nobutada (1557–82), who also committed suicide rather than be captured. As soon as news of the assassinations reached Hideyoshi, he acted with alacrity. Calling a truce with his opponents, he raced to Kyoto to hunt down Akechi, killing him only thirteen days later at the battle of Yamazaki. Hideyoshi's action in taking over the Oda forces was viewed by some as presumptuous. Tokugawa Ieyasu, another important daimyō who was later to rule Japan, was touring the Osaka region when news of the event reached him. Having only a nominal bodyguard, he prudently retreated to his home province making it clear he disapproved of Hideyoshi's action, an attitude that ultimately lead to open hostility between them.

After some initial delay caused by bad weather, the Tenshō mission finally set sail from Nagasaki on 20 February 1582, travelling first to Macao where the continuing bad weather obliged them to stay until rather late in year. Eventually they landed in Goa where Father Valignano left the group. After numerous adventures, including an unplanned landing in Africa caused by inept navigation, they landed in Lisbon on 11 August 1584. Travelling first to Coimbra, the party made their way to Madrid via Toledo. At the royal palace the group had an audience with Philip II, presenting him with letters from various Japanese dignitaries and numerous gifts, among which were armours, weapons, horse harness, painted screens and lacquer work. It is generally accepted that there were two armours among the gifts,[5] an assumption based on an inventory taken in that year of Philip's 'Treasure House' in the palace. The first document is dated 13 June 1585 and describes:

---

5   J. A. Abranches Pinto et al., *La première ambassade du Japon en Europe* (Tokyo, 1942), 87, 88.

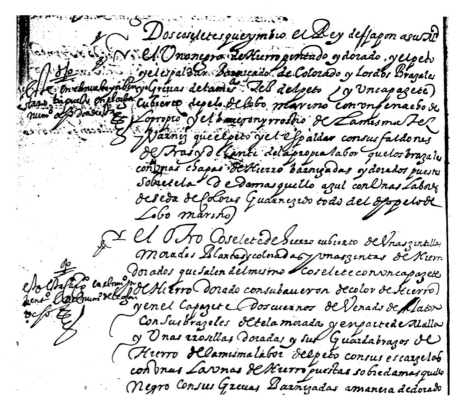

Two armours, given to his Majesty by the King of Japan.

The one of black steel painted and gilded, with a breastplate and the shoulder guards red ribboned and the two sleeves and the greaves of splints […] as the breast, and a helmet covered with fur, with a crest belonging, with a neck guard of lames of similar work, varnished like the breast and the shoulder guards, with its fauld of lames of similar form, the sleeves with a few plates of iron varnished and gilded and sewn onto a damask of blue silk and colours, […] garnished also with seal fur [*pelo de lobo marino*, see figure 1].

The description of the hair covering on the helmet positively identifies it as being the *zunari kabuto,* or head-shaped helmet, that survived in Madrid until a fire in 1884 destroyed all but the iron bowl (figure 2). It was a helmet designed to look like a human head with embossed eyes and eyebrows on the peak, applied ears, and a covering of bear bristles embedded in lacquer. Helmets of this type were not uncommon at this period and often depicted particular hairstyles, although the embossed

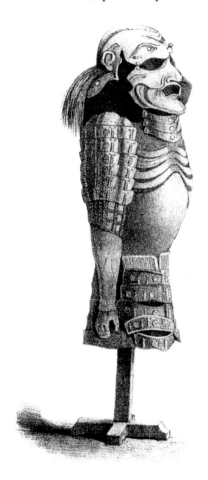
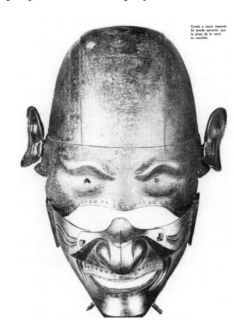

Figure 2 Left, one of two armours preserved in the Real Amería in Madrid, as drawn in Jubinal's catalogue of 1840
Right, the helmet originally covered with hair is still identifiable
(Real Armería, Madrid E.136, Patrimonio Nacional)

eyes are a novel feature. A nineteenth-century drawing shows that the *shikoro* or neck guard of this helmet was also covered with longer yak hair that hung over the plates.[6] The helmet is described as having a crest. This is now missing but two small rivet holes on the brow plate show that an attachment for it once existed. The description also states that other parts of the armour were also decorated with fur. This would refer to the fact that some armours have the lower plates of various elements fringed with bear fur to help shed rain. None of the surviving armours known to have been in Europe during the sixteenth or seventeenth century have this feature so we must assume this armour, other than its helmet, is now lost or is unrecognized.

By the nineteenth century, when for the first time drawings and photographs of the Japanese armours in Madrid were published, the

---

6   A. Jubinal, and G. Sensi, *La Armeria Reale* (Paris, 1840).

various elements of the three armours had become very mixed. The hair-covered helmet had become associated, quite logically to European eyes, with a cuirass modelled on a human torso, with breasts, ribs and spinal protrusions and known in Japanese as a *nio dō*. The origin of this cuirass, or *dō* in Japanese, is discussed later.

The second armour listed in the inventory is described:

> The other armour is covered with purple, white and red ribbons and plates of gilded steel that make up the cuirass, with a helmet of gilded steel with its bevor of natural colour and on the helmet two horns of brass. The sleeves of purple cloth partly of mail and a few gilded plates and its shoulder guards of steel lames in ranks. The breast is continued with tassets of black-varnished scales and the greaves with coloured ribbons [the cloth ties]. It is decorated with lions.

This armour can be positively identified with various fragments of armour that survived the fire by reason of the applied ornaments of copper gilt in the form of Chinese lions, *shishi*, on most of the major plates (figure 3). Some of the fragments retain their lacing in purple and white confirming the identification. In addition to the shishi, this armour is also decorated with applied heraldic badges, *kamon*, often just *mon* in English, that identified the owner. They were often stylized flowers, applied in gilded copper in this case in the form of *kirimon*, three pawlonia tree leaves with a pattern of 3–5–3 flowers, and chrysanthemums, *kikumon*, of twelve petals. Again, by the nineteenth century when the surviving Madrid armours were illustrated, this dō had gained a helmet bowl, sleeves and other elements that were not its own. In the drawings and photographs it is shown with a sixty-two-plate helmet bowl with numerous small standing rivets on each of the plates, described in Japanese as a *ko boshi bachi*. It is clear from the nineteenth-century drawing that the helmet bowl was not attached to the neck guard, being simply put together for display. The reason for the confusion no doubt arose because this bowl has a shishi painted in lacquer on the centre of the peak. To the right of the shishi is a kirimon, but in this case with a 7–9–7 arrangement of flowers, and on the left a sixteen-petalled kikumon. These kamon had been reserved for the exclusive use of the emperor until Hideyoshi was granted their use and given the name Toyotomi on his appointment as regent over a

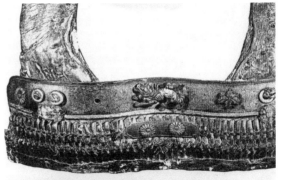

Figure 3   The second armour from Philip II's Treasure House (Real Armería, Madrid E.133, Patrimonio Nacional)

unified Japan in 1585. These same Imperial kamon also occur lacquered on some of the plates of the nio dō making it certain that this ko boshi bachi originally belonged with that cuirass.

In the same nineteenth-century images, the nio dō was again quite logically mounted with a pair of sleeves and shin guards modelled with muscles and protruding veins. These in fact have the same applied copper gilt kamon that identify them as belonging to the purple white and red cuirass. So, as assembled, the nio dō was drawn and photographed with the wrong helmet, the wrong sleeves and the wrong shin guards. Similarly, the purple, white and red-laced armour is depicted with the wrong helmet bowl and wrong limb armour. Since Hideyoshi was not granted the 7–9–7 kirimon and sixteen-petalled kikumon heraldry until some three years after the Tensho Mission had sailed, the nio dō and the ko boshi helmet bowl did not arrive in Spain with that mission. The inventory description states that the purple, white and red-laced armour had a gold-lacquered helmet, almost certainly the rather conical multi-plate bowl with a flat peak that still survives in Madrid. This helmet bowl, of thirty-two plates with standing flanges, has small ornamental decorative plaques at the base of each plate, known as *igaki*.

It is at this point perhaps worth describing something about the armour worn in Japan at this period. Prior to the period of the civil wars all armour was lamellar, that is, composed of numerous small plates (lamellae) made of iron or rawhide laced together, the whole being almost totally covered by the silk lacing that held the rows of lamellae together. These armours were costly to produce and very much the prerogative of the wealthy. While effective against swords, spears and arrows, lamellar armours proved to be no protection against bullets that shattered the scales and forced fragments into the wound. Plate armour, although developed before the introduction of guns, was found to be more resistant to penetration and also distributed the energy of a bullet over a wider area, limiting the traumatic shock. Despite this, those of higher rank still had lamellar armours made in the older styles for wear on formal occasions. These formal armours were a speciality of the Iwai group of Nara that lies in the Kansai area surrounding Kyoto, and hence are referred to as Kansai style armours. Many of the armours that reached Europe were in fact made by Iwai Yozaemon who signed his work in red lacquer on the inside of the breast and inside the neck guard. Because several of these armours were sent to Europe as gifts by Tokugawa Ieyasu, it has become an accepted fact that Yozaemon was Ieyasu's personal armourer. However, since some of these armours can be identified by the heraldry on them as having belonged to people Ieyasu had defeated in battle, it is more likely that most were the spoils of war.

The same manuscript inventory in the Spanish archives shows that another armour was included in the gift.[7] The second document preserved in Madrid relating to the 1585 gift is an order, dated 1603, to transfer various items from the Treasure House to the Royal Armoury following the death of Philip II. Among the items is a Japanese armour described as:

---

7 A. Soler del Campo, Real Armería, Madrid, personal communication.

A black corselet with its sleeves and shoulder guards of plates garnished with a mesh of black ribbons having an attachment of gilded brass on its sleeves and four others opposed on the front and back.

A black morion of the same, with a mask and a crest of gilded leather and in the centre a gold cross on a green field and in front two tufts of black hair, and a *baruas* [?] in black and white (figure 4)

At this time the Real Armería was furnished with large cupboards in which armours were stored. A marginal note alongside this description states that the armour was placed in location 8 with the two armours described in the 1585 inventory. Clearly at some date between 1585 and 1603 the two armours originally kept in the Treasure House had been exchanged with this one. This third armour can be identified with confidence as one that appears later in the story. Unlike the other two armours in the gift, it is in a severe, practical fighting style from the second half of the sixteenth century. The 'attachments of gilded brass' and the 'gold cross' mentioned in the description refer to ornamental plaques held in place by gilt rivets engraved with the kamon of the Shimazu family that occur on various parts of the armour. The most likely donor of this gift, which shows battle damage, is Ōtomo Sōrin who is known to have fought the Shimazu.

Following their meeting with Philip II, the Japanese party travelled to Alicante where they boarded a ship for Livorno, travelling from there to Florence. In that city they met Francisco de Medici (1541–87) who is reported to have received a gift of two armours.[8] Quoted in this reference is a description from an inventory of the Medici armoury carried out in 1613. One of the armours given to Francisco is listed as:

> *Una armadura di legnio indiano cioe petto estience listrato d'oro ordini con girello fatto a scarcelle semile e manchi di tela near con pui pezzi.*

This description is somewhat difficult to interpret but clearly indicates the armour had a gold lacquered 'breastplate' in layers and that a 'spiral' (*girello*) was involved. Unusually there is no mention of a helmet, mask or shoulder guards, although the description does include the reference to 'other pieces'. It is almost certain that the two armours given to the Medici eventually found their way to Copenhagen; a supposition examined later.

Rudolf II of Bohemia (1552–1612), like many of his contemporaries, collected thousands of strange and wonderful objects for his cabinet of curiosities' housed in his vast castle in Prague. The collection grew so large that he finally had to build a new wing to house it. His paternal uncle was Philip II of Spain and as a youth he had lived at the devoutly Catholic Spanish court. Later in his life, although technically the Holy Roman Emperor, he grew tolerant of other religions including Protestantism. An inventory of Prague Castle made in 1607–11 includes two Japanese armours. Tradition has it that they were a gift to the Habsburg Court and the date proves that they can only have arrived in Europe with the Tenshō mission. The mission itself did not travel to Prague, and at this stage in his life Rudolf was a recluse, suffering periods of depression and being very reluctant to travel. It would seem the Jesuits advisors to the mission felt that the Holy Roman Emperor was sufficiently important to have warranted such a gift and had deposited the two armours in Madrid to be sent on to Prague.

The inventory reads:

---

8 M. Scalini, 'Exotica in der mediceischen Kunstkammer' in H. Trnek (ed.) *Exotica: Portugals Entdeckungen im Spiegel fürstlicher Kunst- und Wunderkammern der Renaissance* (Mainz, 2001), 128–43.

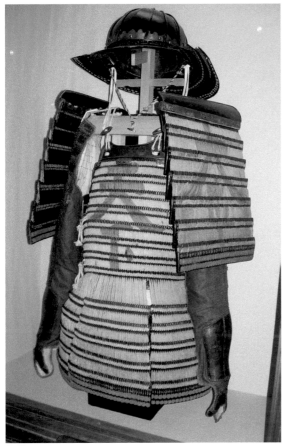
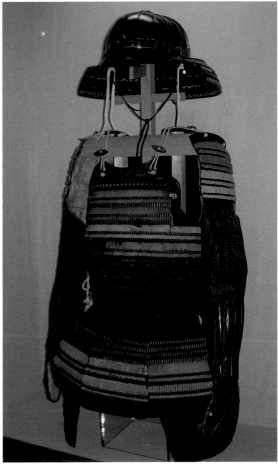

1 indianische rüstung, von leüchter materii, mit schwartzem glantzetem lacc überzogen, brustharnisch, hutt und kinstuckh in einer grossen schiebladen oder trühlein.

1 andere dergleichen indianische rüstung, etwas stärcker und mehr geziert, von seydenwerck und etwas von metall oder messing dabey, sonsten auch schwartz gelact, in gleichmessigem trülin mit ein fürschieber.[9]

Figure 5   The two armours listed in the 1603 inventory of Prague Castle, now in Schloss Ambras in Austria (Kunsthistorisches Museum, Vienna, AM PA.586–7, photographs by Thom Richardson)

Following Rudolf's death much of the Kunstkammer was sold off to pay off the huge debts he had run up. Further depredations of

---

9   M. Pfaffenbichler, Kunsthistoriches Museum, Vienna, personal communication. R. Bauer and H. Haupt, 'Das Kunstkammer Inventar Kaiser Rudolfs II: ein Inventar aus den Jahren 1607–11', *Jahrbuch der Kunsthistorischen Sammlungen in Wien* 72 (1976), 1–191, at pl. 42, nos 746–7.

the collection followed during the Thirty Years War. After various vicissitudes, during which the two armours were displayed in Brussels as the armours of Montezuma and that of his son, they were finally returned to Central Europe and are now housed in Schloss Ambras in Austria.[10] Both of these armours are in the formal Kansai style, with *akodanari* helmet bowls, large spreading neck guards, *dō maru*, the lamellar armour that wraps around the body with the opening under the right arm, or *kebiki* laced *ni mai dō* which is similar to a dō maru but is hinged under the left arm and large shoulder guards. One has the characters *tenka*, or 'below heaven' worked in red in the white lacing on the breast and *sode*, shoulder guards. It bears an unidentified kamon of wisteria leaves and flowers on the plates of the forearm indicating it belonged to a family who claimed descent from the Fujiwara clan. The other armour is one of twelve similar ones, in this case laced in red, white and brown that belonged to Hideyoshi. These armours are said to have been worn by Hideyoshi's doubles or *kagemusha* on the battlefield, but were more likely to have been for his personal guards. Eleven similar armours from this series, some having blue instead of brown lacing in the waist region, are distributed in various Japanese collections.[11] All of these armours are decorated in gold lacquer with the familiar *kirimon* with 3–5–3 flowers used by Hideyoshi before he became regent.

*

Following their stay in Florence the four youths travelled to Rome, where they were presented to Pope Gregory VIII, and after his death, to Pope Sixtus V. Among the gifts recorded as being given to the pontiff was a screen decorated with a painting of Azuchi castle sent by Oda Nobunaga. Leaving Rome the group travelled around northern Italy, visiting Venice where they presented a letter to the doge written by Mancio Ito. The mission then moved on to Turin. Once again an armour seems to have been given as a gift. A small drawing of an armour appears in the 1840 catalogue of the dynastic armoury in Turin (figure 6).[12] Unfortunately there is no indication of the armour's origins but it is clear from the drawing that it is yet another of the formal

---

10 Kunsthistorisches Museum, *Sammlungen Schloss Ambras, Die Rustkammer* (Vienna, 1981), pls 31, 32.

11 Exhibition catalogue, Nara Prefectural Museum, *Nara katchu shiten Osaka Castle* (Nara Ken Bijutsukan, 1987), 35–9.

12 V. Seyssel d'Aix, *Armeria Antica e Moderna di S. M. Carlo Alberto* (Turino, 1840) 20, 1.16 pl.5

armours in the Kansai style with the usual spreading neck guard and large shoulder guards. In 1898 a lavish photographic record of some of the major items from the Turin collection was published and this armour is illustrated, mounted on a stuffed horse with a late Edo period harness.[13] Unfortunately the photograph is such that the kamon that might identify the armour more positively cannot be made out. Also in this publication is a photograph of another helmet and mask from about 1580 as well as a late Edo period dō-maru armour; the latter obviously acquired by the duke after the opening of Japan in 1853. By 1898 three Japanese armours are listed in the catalogue of the Turin armoury but the lack of illustrations and the brief descriptions, make it impossible to reach any meaningful conclusions. All that can

Figure 6   Gift armours in the Armeria Reale, Turin Left, the standing armour in the 1840 catalogue Right, the equestrian armour in the 1898 catalogue

---

13 Armeria Reale, *Armeria Antiqua e Moderna di S. M. il Reyd'italia, Torino* (Turin, 1898), vol. I.

be said is that during the period between the publication of the 1840 catalogue and that of 1898, two more Japanese armours, nos 53 and 54, had been added to the Turin collection. It is known that the duke was at this time adding items to his dynastic collection, buying many of the items on the Parisian art market. The first of these new armours in the 1898 catalogue is described as complete and is almost certainly the nineteenth-century dō-maru. The other is described as being for use on foot and as being incomplete and different from the other two. Just what prompted the author to this description is not known, but it must be this armour to which the second photographed helmet belonged. A possible source for this armour is discussed later. On a recent visit to the museum the only pieces of Japanese armour of any kind that could be found were two helmets, one that belonging to the dō-maru and the second helmet from the photographic catalogue. What happened to the remainder of the armours and when they were lost from the collection is not known.

The Tenshō mission returned to Japan on 21 July 1590, staying in India for several years for fear of the edict against Christianity imposed by Hideyoshi who was now ruling Japan as regent. The mission brought back gifts for Hideyoshi, ostensibly from the governor of Goa, but probably on the orders of the Spanish king who would have learned of his appointment as reagent from the Jesuits. These included two gilded armours, pistols and a campaign tent. Although the gifts do not appear to have survived, the illuminated letter accompanying them is now in the Myoho-in, Kyoto.[14] In 1598 Philip II died leaving the Spanish throne to his son Philip III (1578–1621). Even before his death his father had reservations about his son's fitness to rule. These fears were justified since as soon as he was seated on the throne Philip III entrusted the running of the country to the Duke of Lerma and embarked on a life of pleasure, spending vast amounts of money on festivities, and it must be said, works of piety.

As mentioned above, two Japanese armours that appeared in Denmark during the seventeenth century are now preserved in the Royal Danish Kunstkammer where they first appear in the inventory of 1689 (Eab 31 and Eab 32).[15] Christian IV (1588–1648), like Rudolf of

---

14 Watanabe, *The World and Japan*, catalogue no. 72
15 B. Dam Mikkelsen and T. N. D. Lundaek, *Ethnographic Objects in the Royal Danish Kunstkammer 1650–1800* (Copenhagen, 1980), 248

Bohemia, was a passionate collector of the unusual, employing agents all over Europe to find objects for his cabinet of curiosities. Because the Danes had no involvement with the Japanese at this time, it is clear that the armours had been acquired from some country that did. As has already been speculated, these two armours must have been acquired from the Medici.

One of these armours, in the formal Kansai style, is lacquered in gold, a feature that accords with the description of the armour in the Medici inventory. It bears a kamon formed of three comma shapes arranged in a circular formation, a variation of the *mitsu tomoe maru kamon* that was almost certainly the inspiration for the term 'spiral' in the Medici description. Although many families used this kamon, the comma shapes on this armour have very small heads similar to the version used by the Kuki family. Traditionally the Kuki had been sea-farers with a rather unsavoury reputation for piracy, operating from a base on Kyushu, later becoming more respectable and joining the forces of Oda Nobunaga. This would accord with it having been donated by a Kyushu daimyō.

The other armour in Copenhagen is a practical fighting armour of the late Muromachi or Momoyama period with a black lacquered, smooth faced cuirass known as a *hotoke dō*, the name alluding to the fact that the surface is unblemished and hence likened to the Buddha. It has now lost its helmet, mask and leg defences, but these are shown in a painting by Jan Bruegel the Younger (1601–78) and Hendrick van Balen (1575–1632) entitled *Allegory of Touch* preserved in the Musée Calvet, Avignon.[16] The Japanese armour can be seen on a stand behind the pile of European armour in the left foreground. This same assembly of armour parts, but without the Japanese armour, appears in several of Bruegel's paintings, such as that in the Uffizi Gallery in Florence entitled *Allegory of Air and Fire*, no. 1204, dated to later in his life. Bruegel may have owned the European armours and used them repeatedly as studio props, but the similarity of their arrangement in all of the paintings suggests that he was copying the details from a sketch or preliminary study. Bruegel is known to have travelled in Italy and may have seen and drawn the Japanese armour while in Florence.

Alternatively he may have sketched the armour and included it

---

16 W. J. Karcheski, 'Hammerman of the Gods', *Royal Armouries Yearbook* 4 (1999), 42.

Figure 7 'Allegory of Touch' by Jan Bruegel the Younger (1601–78) and Hendrick van Balen (1575–1632), painted about 1630 (Musée Calvet, Avignon, 827.5.24)

in the painting because it was regarded as a novelty on its arrival in Antwerp where Bruegel had his studio. If the latter supposition were correct, it would establish the date of its transfer to Copenhagen as being around 1630. Evident in the Bruegel painting is the fact that the armour originally had an *etchu zunari kabuto,* a form of helmet with a peak in front, and splinted sleeves, both black lacquered like the rest.

The Tensho mission distributed some eight armours around Europe: two to Rudolf II of Bohemia, two to the Medici who appear to have subsequently sold them to the Danish court, one to the Duke of Savoy and three to the Spanish court.

*

Following the visit to Spain by the four Japanese youths, other maritime nations of Europe began to take notice of the potential for trade in the Far East. In 1598 a fleet of five ships with a total crew of 507 left Rotterdam to trade in the Moluccas. By the time they had crossed the Atlantic many of the crew were dead from hunger or disease. For five months the fleet attempted to round Cape Horn but only four ships were eventually successful, the *Geloof* (*Faith*) giving up and returning to Holland. Following that ordeal, another ship was captured by the Spanish and a third set off alone to the Moluccas where the crew were murdered. The two remaining ships made their way across the Pacific but lost contact in a storm during which the *Hoop* (*Hope*) sank leaving the *Liefde* (*Charity*) to sail on alone. After terrible hardships the ship finally made landfall in Japan, in the province of Bungo, in 1600. On board were twenty-three Dutch and the English pilot, William Adams. So weak and diseased were the crew that six died before they could be nursed back to health. The Dutch survivors were eventually allowed to leave, taking with them a letter giving them permission to trade, but Adams did not leave with them. During the same year that the Dutch reached Japan, the short-lived peace the country had enjoyed under Hideyoshi began to break down. Hideyoshi had died in 1598, leaving his five-year-old son Hideyori in the care of both civil and military guardians. Tokugawa Ieyasu, one of five military guardians, saw Adams as a useful source of information about Europe and, because he was a Protestant, a counter to the Jesuit priests and other Catholics. Adams was never allowed to return to England and was ultimately made one of Ieyasu's retainers, being given an estate and a Japanese wife with whom he had children.

Inevitably a struggle for power broke out among the guardians of Hideyori (1593–?1614) culminating in the largest battle fought on Japanese soil at the small village of Seki ga Hara in 1600 that involved some 120,000 men. Ieyasu emerged as victor, helped it is said by cannon salvaged by Adams from the *Liefde*. With no opposition, Ieyasu was made shōgun in 1603 but he passed the title to his son Hidetada just three years later and retired to Sumpu, now Shizuoka, where he continued to wield considerable power.

Spurred on by the success of the Dutch, a group of English merchants founded the Honourable East India Company (HEIC) in 1600 to finance trading expeditions to Asia. They were followed a few years later by the Dutch, who put their trading voyages on a more official footing by establishing the Vereenigde Oost-Indische Compagnie (VOC) in 1602. As soon as news reached Holland that permission had been granted to trade with the Japanese, a VOC ship was dispatched, reaching the island of Hirado in 1609 where a trading station was established importing goods from both the East Indies and Europe. In 1611 the VOC's

Figure 8   Picture by Jacob van Campen (1596–1657) The armour shown is now in the Musée de l'Armée in Paris (http://oud. digischool.nl/ckv2/ burger/burger17de/ huistenbosch/ oranjezaal3a.jpg)

representative in Japan, Jacques Specx, and his deputy, Pieter Sergerz, travelled to Edo with a letter from Stadholder Mauritz and presents for the shōgun, Tokugawa Hidetada. In return Hidetada presented Mauritz Van Nassau with various gifts, among which were three armours.[17] These armours were eventually installed in the Huis den Bosch in The Hague, one being depicted in a triumphal painting by Jacob van Campen (1596–1657).[18] Again the armour depicted is in the Kansai style with an *akodanari* helmet bowl, large neck guard and large shoulder guards. The *fukigayeshi*, or 'turn-backs' of the helmet display the sixteen-petalled kikumon and the 7–9–7 kirimon granted to Toyotomi Hideyoshi in 1585, in this case done in gold lacquer and placed side by side.[19]

In 1611 the HEIC finally dispatched an expedition of three ships to the Spice Islands of South East Asia via the Cape of Good Hope. They were commanded by Captain John Saris (1580–1643) who had orders to proceed to Japan if he was unable to fill all three ships. Arriving late in the season, Saris was only able to fill two of his ships with spices so, acting as his orders dictated, he sailed on in the ship *Clove*, arriving at

---

17 O. Nachod, *Die Bezeihungen der Niederländischen Ostindischen Kompanie zu Japan im siebzehnten Jahrhundert* (Berlin, 1897), 147, 148.

18 K. N. D. Zandvliet, Rijksmuseum, personal communication.

19 B. Le Dauphin, 'Trente ans déjà', *Bulletin Association Franco-Japonaise* 69 (June 2000), 25, 27.

the island of Hirado in 1613. On his arrival he was entertained by the local lord, Matsura Shigenobu, better known by his Buddhist name Hōin. As was common in Japan, Hōin had passed the title of daimyō to his grandson but still held on to power and running things from behind the scenes. Being totally unfamiliar with Japanese society and its protocols, Saris thought Hōin was the 'King' of Japan and gave him a lavish gift that included large quantities of cloth, silverware and a pair of gold decorated guns that are described as being 'double locked'. Being unsure what to do about the arrival of the English, Hōin sent word to Edo asking the Tokugawa government how he should proceed. While waiting for the reply, Saris tried desperately to keep his sailors occupied to prevent them from escaping ashore and

Figure 9   Two of the armours given to Mauritz of Nassau. Captured by the French about 1795 and taken to Paris (Musée de l'Armée Paris G.754 and G.758.2)

21

running amok. To this end, on the 25 July, he decided to celebrate the anniversary of King James's coronation, writing in his diary:

> I ordered eleven pieces ordnance to be shot off, our ship to abroad all her gallantry, which the naturals took great notice of, the King [Hōin] much commending our order in remembering our duty. And in the afternoon visiting his majesty at his court, he bestowed on me a fair armour, which he said he would give at this present for he held it of some esteem, having worn it in the wars of Corea.[20]

On receiving news of the arrival of the English, Ieyasu dispatched Adams with instructions to escort Saris to Edo to meet the shōgun. At their first meeting Saris notes in his diary that Adams had 'gone native', dressing in Japanese clothes, refusing to sleep on the ship and being distant with his countrymen. Nevertheless, he assisted Saris in selecting suitable gifts for Ieyasu and the shōgun, as well as instructing him on the protocol of the shōgun's court. On their way to Edo they stopped at Sumpu, Ieyasu's retirement home, where Saris again gave him presents of cloth, guns and silverware. Ieyasu tried to persuade Saris to set up the English trading station near to Edo but Saris declined and insisted on staying on Hirado. Following this courtesy call, Saris travelled on to Edo where he met with the shōgun who granted the English permission to trade. As was required, gifts were exchanged, those from Saris being noticeably inferior to those given to Ieyasu. In return Saris was given two armours for James I. He records in his diary:

> And towards evening the King sent 2 varnished Armours, a present to his Majesty the King of England, Allso a Tach (which none weare there but souldiers of the best ranke) and a wagadash a present from him to my selfe.[21]

As Saris was a merchant and therefore not entitled to wear a long sword, it is appropriate that he should be given a *wakizashi*.[22] Back in Hirado, Saris established a trading station manned by a group of merchants led

---

20 E. Satow, *The Voyage of Captain John Saris to Japan 1613* (London, 1900), 107.
21 Ibid., 134.
22 Members of the military class, the *bushi*, wore two swords, a *katana* with a blade over two feet long and a smaller sword. Other classes including merchants were only permitted to wear a short sword, generally a *wakizashi* having a blade between one and two feet long.

by Richard Cocks, and left for England calling at the Spice Islands on the way home.

Officers of the HEIC were strictly forbidden to indulge in private trade but, like most captains, Saris ignored this edict, filling the ship with spices he bought privately. At a subsequent enquiry one sailor described how Saris would fill the space in the bread room with spices as soon as a loaf was withdrawn. On their arrival in England the *Clove* docked at Plymouth rather than in London, giving Saris an opportunity to unload his illegal cargo away from the prying eyes of the Company. When he finally did reach the capital the ship was seized and searched. To the disgust of the Company, who had already charged Saris with financial irregularities, a quantity of Japanese pornography was found among his belongings, which were secretly burned at night. Saris was dismissed in disgrace, retiring to the borough of Fulham in London where he lived comfortably for the rest of his life on the proceeds of his journey.

The two armours given to James I are in the usual Kansai style and are signed by Iwai Yozaemon of Nara. One was deposited in the armoury at the Tower of London, the other being housed in one of the royal palaces. Following the execution of Charles I, much of the royal art collection was sold off to the public, the administration of this process being assigned to the poet and musician George Wither.[23] Among the paintings, furniture and other treasures was the Japanese armour now in the Royal Collection. It was bought by a Major Bass for the then considerable sum of £10.[24] After the restoration of the monarchy, the armour, along, with much of the art that had been sold off, was recovered and returned to the Royal Collection where it still remains (as AL.27.11 on loan to the Royal Armouries). This armour is somewhat eclectic, consisting of disparate pieces, lacquered and laced to match, although the helmet and dō undoubtedly belong together since they both bear Iwai Yozaemon's signature. There are no kamon, their place being taken by dragons and clouds in gold lacquer; presumably because the armourer tasked with putting the ensemble together was unsure as to James I's heraldry.

---

23 A. Pritchard, 'George Wither and the Sale of the Estate of Charles I', *Modern Philology*, 77, no. 4 (May 1980), 370–81.
24 A. MacGregor, *The Late King's Goods* (London, 1989), 353–4.

Figure 10   Armour given to James I by Tokugawa Hidetada. It is by Iwai Yozaemon and belonged to Takeda Katsuyori, whose mon is also shown (Royal Armouries XXVI.AI)

The other armour (XXVIA.I, figure 10) remained in the Tower of London, gradually becoming more dilapidated over the centuries. It was returned to Japan in the 1970s where it was repaired and re-laced. Although polishing has obliterated much of the gold lacquered decoration, one complete kamon remains showing that the armour originally belonged to the Takeda family. It is far too small to have fitted the famous daimyō Takeda Shingen, who was rather corpulent in his later life, and probably belonged to his son Katsuyori. The acquisition of the armour is consistent with the fact that Tokugawa Ieyasu conquered the Takeda homelands in the province of Kai in 1582, when he presumably captured the armour with other Takeda possessions. Of the armour given to Saris by Matsura Hōin, and the wakizashi given to him by Tokugawa Hidetada, no trace can now be found. Nothing Japanese is listed in Saris's will, despite the fact that he was presented with a *naginata* and given other weapons by various daimyō who visited him during his stay on Hirado.

Having failed to persuade the Protestant traders to operate in the Kanto area, Ieyasu devised another scheme to wrest the European trade from the Kyushu daimyō. Plans were made to send another delegation to Spain, this time on the pretext of asking for more missionaries to preach in the Edo area. In reality Ieyasu wanted to persuade the Jesuits to move their trading base to the Kantō region around Edo, and to gain permission to trade with Mexico and South America. The task of planning this expedition was tasked to Ieyasu's retainer, Date Masamune of Sendai (1567–1636), the instruction being transmitted through the Minister of the Navy, Mukai Shogen. The person chosen by Date Masamune to lead the delegation was Hasekura Rokuemon Tsunenaga (1571–1622), the son of a minor vassal who had been executed for a misdemeanour. Put simply, Tsunenaga was given the choice of accepting command of the mission or suffering the same fate as his father.

While the planning went on in Sendai, Mukai Shogen and Will Adams began work on a ship to transport the party across the Pacific. To this end some 800 shipwrights, 3,000 carpenters and 700 blacksmiths were put to work. Initially named *Date Maru*, the ship was completed in only forty-five days. By the 28 October 1613 the ship, now renamed as *San Juan Bautista*, captain Sebastian Vizciano, sailed with Father Luis Sotelo, Hasekura Tsunenaga, twelve Tokugawa samurai, some 140 Japanese merchants, servants and sailors and around forty other Europeans. Also on board was Tanaka Shosuke, a metal dealer, who had undertaken an exploratory trip to Mexico in 1610, on the orders of Ieyasu. This expedition is known as the Keicho mission from the year in which it sailed. After an uneventful crossing of the Pacific, the ship arrived at Acapulco on 25 January 1614. From there the Japanese party travelled to Mexico City, where the greater number stayed to trade. Hasekura and his party travelled on in a Spanish ship to Havana and finally to Spain where the group landed in October 1614 and began making its way towards Madrid. During the journey the delegation passed through Seville where it is recorded that Hasekura presented the mayor with a *daisho*, a matching pair of swords.

The meeting with Philip III took place on the 30 January 1615 when letters from the Shōgun Tokugawa Hidetada and Date Masamune were presented along with numerous gifts. Only one of the armours given to the Spanish by Hasekura Tsunenaga can be identified with any certainty. This is the armour with the nio dō that was later to become associated with the fur covered helmet and the limb armour modelled with muscles. This must be one of Toyotomi Hideyoshi's armours since no other person would have dared use the imperial heraldry with which it is decorated. Just why Ieyasu chose to give Hideyoshi's armours to the Europeans can only be speculation but we know that he gave two to the Dutch and at least one to the Spanish. One possibility is that the *kami* or spirit of a dead person was thought to be associated with his armour. By shipping them to Europe, the spirit of his old adversary was about as far removed from Japanese soil as it was possible to get.

While the mission was in Spain, fighting broke out yet again in Japan. Toyotomi Hideyori, Hideyoshi's son, was now of age and was attracting support from those still loyal to the Toyotomi cause and from those who had been defeated at Seki ga Hara. This threat to Tokugawa rule was resolved in 1613 and 1614 by two attacks on the Toyotomi stronghold of Osaka Castle.

In addition to the armours given to Philip III, others were deposited at the Spanish court as gifts for Henry IV of France,[25] a clear indication that Ieyasu was attempting to establish diplomatic relations with the other great powers in Europe. We know that Philip complied with the request and forwarded the armours to the French in due course because a Japanese armour appears in the inventory of the French royal collection taken in 1673. The entry reads:

No. 337   Une armure à l'indienne de carton, escorce d'arbre et cuir, lassez de soye et verny de la Chine.[26]

---

25 Takauji, Nikko Toshogu Shrine, personal communication. The record is in the archive at the shrine.

26 J. Guiffrey, *Inventaire général du mobilier de la couronne sous Louis XV (1663–1715)* (Paris, 1886), part II, 83. S. V. Grancsay, *Master French Gunsmith Designs* (New York, 1970), 202.

The references to cardboard and bark suggest that the clerk was struggling to describe the totally unfamiliar lacquered rawhide from which most of the armour was made. The fact that the armour is described as being lacquered and laced with silk precludes it from being anything else but Japanese. By coincidence the 1673 inventory stops at item no. 337, possibly because it was abandoned, or more likely because subsequent pages are missing. In the 1729 inventory, which is complete, two more armours, numbered 379 and 380, are described with exactly the same words. In fact no. 380 is a genuine Indian armour from Rajasthan dating to the seventeenth century.[27] The two Japanese armours given by Tokugawa Ieyasu are now displayed in the Musée de l'Armée in Paris (figure 11) together with two of the armours that had

Figure 11 The two armours, plus swords and staff weapons appear in the inventory of the French Royal Collection (Musee de l'Armée, Paris G758.1 and G753)

27 S. V. Grancsay, *Master French Gunsmith Designs* (New York, 1970), 203

Figure 12   The armour with the kamon of the Mori family in a painting on ceiling of the Hall of Mirrors in Versailles

been given to the Dutch, looted by French revolutionary troops from the Hague in 1795. Both of the two armours from Ieyasu to the French are in the usual Kansai style made by Iwai Yozaemon of Nara. One is decidedly composite with the various elements having different kamon. The kamon on the other French armour is a stylized crane formed into a circle. The bird is depicted as being much more attenuated than later renderings, but almost certainly a kamon used by the Mori family.[28] This armour occurs in a painting done in 1687 by Le Brun (1619–90), on the ceiling of the Hall of Mirrors in the palace of Versailles.[29]

Other items listed in the inventory of the French Royal collection can be identified as Japanese, in particular a naginata and several swords. The former is described in the inventory:

> *274 Une hallebard dont le bois est verny de la Chine par le hault le fer en manière de coustelas.*[30]

Among the swords listed in the inventory are:

28 Le Dauphin, 'Trente ans déjà', 24, 26.
29 N. Milovanovic, *La Gallery des Glaces: Charles Le Brun Maître d'Oeuvre Chateau de Versailles* (Paris, 2007).
30 Guiffrey (1886), part II, 77. S. V. Grancsay, *Master French Gunsmith Designs* (New York, 1970), 199.

301 Un grand espadon à la tartare, long de quatre pieds quatre pouces, dont la poignée est d'une courroye de cuir, la garde de cuivre toutte unie, le fourreau de bois verny, long de 5 pieds.

302 Deux Sabres a la tartare, les poignees de cuir, les guardes de cuivres avec ornemens aussi de cuivre, les fourreaux de bois, l'un verny de noir avec fleurs, l'autre verny de rouge.

303 Un sabre de trois pieds unze pouces de long, a guarde d'argent unie, la poignee de cuir, le fourreau vernis de noir et point blancs.

304 Un petit Sabre de deux pieds, un pouce de long a guarde de fer, poignee de cuir, et fourreau fond noir orne de nacre de perle.[31]

In February 1615 Tsunenaga was baptized in the presence of Philip III as Don Filipe Francisco Hasekura. Travelling to the coast, the party boarded ship and set off for Italy and an audience with Pope Paul V. En route the ship had a forced stopover in St Tropez before reaching Savona where the party changed ship for Italy. On reaching Rome the Japanese finally met the pontiff and again presented letters and gifts. Although the pope agreed to the Japanese request to supply more missionaries he decided that the matter of moving the trade to the Kanto and of trading with Mexico were decisions that had to be taken by the Spanish king. Back in Spain Philip turned down both of these requests, using as his excuse that the Tokugawa were not the kings of Japan. In reality news had reached Spain that the Tokugawa were becoming less tolerant of Catholicism and persecutions of Catholics had begun.

Having failed in its main purpose, the Keicho mission left Spain, travelling back to Japan via Mexico and the Philippines where Hasekura acquired a kris and a kastana[32] as gifts for Date Masamune. The ship finally reached Nagasaki in August 1620 only to find that Catholicism had been proscribed. Tokugawa Ieyasu was now dead and there was already a mood abroad that the foreigners should be expelled and the country closed off to all foreign influence. Although the kris and kastana seems to have pleased Masamune, two other gifts proved less than successful. One was a portrait of the Pope and the

---

31 Grancsay, *Master French Gunsmith Designs*, 200.
32 K. Sasaki, 'The Kastane and Kris', *Royal Armouries Yearbook*, 3 (1998), 141–4.

other a painting of Hasekura, wearing European costume, praying in front of a crucifix.[33] Tokugawa Hidetada wrote a strongly worded letter to Masamune admonishing him for sending his vassal to Europe and establishing contact with the head of the Catholic Church. Unabashed, Masamune's answering letter points out that he had in fact acted under orders from the Tokugawa themselves, adding that it was they who had paid for the ship, supplied letters to foreign potentates, provided the armours to be given as gifts and supplied twelve samurai as a bodyguard.

Thus ended the second and final diplomatic visit by the Japanese to Europe until the nineteenth century. There were, however, other routes by which Japanese arms and armour reached Europe. Richard Cocks (1566–1624), who had been left behind in Japan by Saris to manage the English Factory, had tried to keep some form of trade going from their base on Hirado. Unfortunately the goods being offered, mainly woollen cloth, were of little interest to the Japanese. In addition, Cocks seems to have been preoccupied in using the Japanese base as a springboard to establish trade with China rather than concentrating on trade with the Japanese. Despite this lack of success the English factory was still required to send a delegation to Edo to renegotiate the trading treaty, and even more importantly to present the shōgun with suitable gifts. On one of these occasions Cocks describes how he was presented with an armour by Tokugawa Hidetada.[34] When the English finally abandoned their factory, this armour would almost certainly be brought to England. It may be the armour illustrated in the picture of the Irish noblemen Sir Neill O'Neill by John Michael Wright (1617–94) painted around 1680 (see figure 13).[35] Wright had spent a decade in Italy in the 1640s and had then served as antiquarian for Archduke Leopold Wilhelm of Austria, Governor of the Spanish Netherlands. Since one of the Dutch armours is unaccounted for, the armour in the painting may alternatively have been obtained from that source. There is no mention of any Japanese items in Wright's will so we do not know whether he owned the armour or had simply borrowed it as a studio prop. He is recorded as having borrowed armour from the

---

33 Sendai Museum (1995), cat no. 166.
34 E. M. Thompson, (ed), *Diary of Richard Cocks* (London, 1883), 179.
35 Tate Gallery, T00132; description at http://www.tate.org.uk/art/artworks/wright-sir-neil-oneill-t00132/text-summary.

Figure 13   Portrait of Sir Neill O'Neill by John Michael Wright painted around 1680 (Tate Images)

Tower of London for that purpose. It seems the Japanese armour had been chosen to emphasize the 'barbaric splendour' of the sitter.

The armour depicted by Wright is interesting. In the painting the gold-lacquered armour, laced in pale blue and white counter-changed in vertical blocks of colour is evidently incomplete. All that appears is the helmet, with the neck guard detached, the cuirass, one shoulder guard and one shin guard. The detached neck guard of the helmet has been sprung around the waist, like the culet of a cuirassier armour, and the shoulder and the shin guard are mocked up to look like an arm defence. In the background a servant holds the helmet bowl fitted with a tuft of feathers in the *tehen kanamono*. A curious feature not seen on any other armour is the presence of small dark blue silk tassels tied at intervals to the lacing. The kamon on the armour is that of the Buddhist 'Wheel of the Law' and may indicate the armour belonged to the Miyake family who were vassals of the Tokugawa based in Mikawa province. The present whereabouts of this armour, if indeed it still exists, is unknown.

The armours that remained in the Real Armería proved to have had an interesting subsequent history. Three of the armours from the Real Armería in Madrid appear in the armoury of the Duke of Infantado at his palace in Guadalajara. Whether the Japanese armours were a gift from Philip III or were purchased by the duke is not known, but the latter is most probable in view of the king's perpetual lack of funds. An inventory of his armoury taken in 1643 lists the three armours as:

> *Mas tres arneses de las Indias, los dos con morriones negros de un barniz, y el otro con un casco dorado; el uno tiene el peto de cuero colorado, y en el espaldar pegada <u>una aljaba para cuatro saetas</u>, y el otro peto es negro, como el morrion, y el otro de seda colores; estos dos arneses tienen dos caranas de los propios arneses, que parecen cuchillas.*[36]

Since the major part of a red-laced armour, that belonged to the hair covered helmet, is no longer in Madrid, it must have been among the armours transferred to Guadalajara. These armours remained in armoury until the occupation of Spain by France during the Napoleonic wars when French troops began the wholesale looting of Spanish art. It would seem that the Duke of Infantado's palace was plundered, the Japanese armour described as having a quiver and four arrows being taken to France. The European armours taken by the French from Spain were deposited in what was then the Musée d'Artillerie, now the Musée de l'Armée, but the Japanese armour from Guadalajara found its way into the collection of François-Joseph Talma (1763–1826). Talma was the son of a Parisian dentist who was sent to England to be educated. On his return to France he practised dentistry himself, becoming increasingly interested in theatricals and eventually joining

---

36 J. S. Rayón and F. de Zalbalburu, *Coleccion de Documentos Ineditos Para La Historia de Espana por El Marques de la Fuensanta del Valle*, vol. 79 (Madrid, 1882), 486.

the Comédie Francaise. He played a significant part in the French Revolution, making friends with many important people. Through his acting he became known to Napoleon who encouraged him in his theatrical career. It was almost certain it was this connection that enabled him to obtain the Japanese armour to add to his considerable collection of exotic costume. Following Talma's death in 1826 an auction sale was held of his art collection.[37] One lot is described as:

> *Une armure indienne avec fleches et corquois.*

The armour was bought by a M. Fatou, a gunsmith working in Paris in the period from 1780 to 1830 who produced many notable arms, including several guns for Napoleon. He is also known to have been a dealer in antique arms and armour and had formed his own collection of choice pieces. On his death his collection was sold and the Japanese armour with its quiver and four arrows is described.[38]

> *Lot 284 Armure Chinoise en vielle laque de chine fixée par des tresse en soie. Ventant de la collection de Talma.*

Who bought the armour from the Fatou sale is unrecorded but it does appear once more in an auction sale held by Maulde & Renou, rue Drouot, Paris 18–23 April 1833 in which it is more fully described:

> *Lot 367 Armure japonaise composée d'un corselet, de tassettes, de brassards, de jambieres et d'un casque en forme de salade avec bavière; le tout lacqué de noir. Elle est accompagnée de son carquois, également laqué et contenant des fleches.*[39]

After this date the armour can no longer be identified in subsequent sales, being lost among the armours arriving in Europe from the newly opened Japan. It is perhaps significant however that it was about this time the Turin armoury of the dukes of Piedmont and Savoy gained its third Japanese armour.

As has already been stated, the history of the armours in the Real Armería, Madrid ended in their partial destruction by fire. We know

---

37 F.-J. Talma, *Catalogues de costumes, tableaux, dessins, gravures, et autre . . . exhibition March* (Paris, 1827).

38 MS copy of arms and armour sold in nineteenth-century French auction sales, Royal Armouries library.

39 Ibid.

that Philip II was given three armours and that Philip III was supposed to have been given three, of which three were sold or given to the Duke of Infantado. The catalogue of the Real Armería for 1793 indicates that the expected three armours remained, catalogued as nos. 212, 213 and 214. The description given is brief and of no value, saying simply that they are 'three very ridiculous armours presented to Philip II by the Emperor of China or the King of Japan'.[40] In 1849 the three armours are listed, 2459, 2489 and 2396.[41] Despite this, during the late nineteenth-century photographs show that there were in fact the expected three armours.

In 1834 Blas Zuloaga (1782–1856) and his son Eusebio (1808–98) from Eibar, both skilled in the decoration of guns and other objects by damascening in gold, were appointed as custodians of the Real Armería in Madrid and tasked with restoring some of the exhibits. Prior to the appointment, Eusebio had received a grant from the Spanish king to spend some time working with Le Page, a Parisian gunmaker. Together Zuloaga and Le Page worked out a scheme to earn themselves a considerable amount of money. Using their position as officials in the pay of the king, the Zuloagas travelled Spain, buying arms and armour from the then impoverished Spanish nobility. These were then shipped to Le Page, who acted as their agent, selling the items on the Parisian art market.[42] Mixed with the legitimate objects was a sprinkling of items, usually minor pieces that would not be missed, stolen from the Real Armería. Before long another agent was found in London but the records of the London auction houses are silent as to whom this might have been. It was in these Paris and London sales that we meet with the remaining two armours from the Duke of Infantado's collection. The first of these appeared in a sale of the Mention and Wagner collection in Paris in 1838:

Lot 230. Armure japonaise – laquée sur fer compose d'un masque en fer laqué en noire, d'un casque avec ornaments et garniture en bronze doré, d'un cuirass épaulieres et tassets formant cuissards, composée de

40 I. Abadia, *Resumen sacado del inventario general historica que se hizo en al ano de 1793. De los arneses, antguos, armes blancas y de fuego con otros efectos de la Real Armería* (Madrid, 1793), 60.

41 J. M. Marcusi, *Catalogo de la Real Armería Madrid* (Madrid, 1849), 172–3, 183, 189.

42 S. Pyhrr, 'Ancient Armour and Arms Recently Received from Spain: Eusebio Zuloaga, Henry LePage and the Real Armería in Spain', *Gladius* 19, (1999) 261–90.

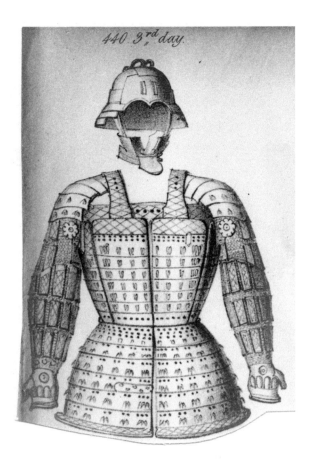

Figure 14 The black-laced armour that was removed from the Treasure House in 1603, illustrated as lot 440 in the Oxenham sale catalogue (Royal Armouries Library)

bandelettes unies entre elles pardes lecets de soie et de guanteletes et brassards dans le même. Cette armoure curreuse est des plus rare.[43]

In another sale, held on 29 April 1841 and the following two days, at Oxenham's rooms in London, was another armour (figure 14) listed as:

Lot 440. A SUIT OF MOORISH ARMOUR believed to be unique, and supposed to have been worn by the MOORS OF GRANADA previous to their expulsion from Spain; the entire suit, (the helmet especially) exhibits a decided approach, in form, to the plate armour of the Europeans; it is composed of blackened steel plates of fine temper, and comprises the helmet, with *metoniere* (mask), back and breast

---

43 *Catalogue d'armes anciennes,* 14 rue des Jeuneurs, Paris, sale of 19–24 March 1838, lot 230.

plates, arms gauntlets and tassets – from the Royal Armoury of Segovia.

Although there had been armour in the royal palace in Segovia in the sixteenth century, it had been transferred to the Real Armería in Madrid by Philip II. The armour in the Oxenham sale, like that in the 1838 sale in Paris, came from the Duke of Infantado's collection and can be identified as that described as having a 'black breastplate like its helmet'.

Unusually for this period, the Oxenham catalogue contained illustrations of some of the principle items, including lot 440, shown in figure 13. From the illustration it is obvious that the armour was in a very dilapidated condition. The artist made numerous mistakes in his attempt to depict this unusual and exotic object. The dō is reversed so that the opening is down the front rather than at the back, the armour being a *haramaki*, literally 'belly wrapper', that opens down the back. The narrow *sei ita* or back plate, made to fit over the opening, has been fitted inside the dō behind the opening. The sode have been mistaken for European style tassets and are shown hung upside down from the waist. Strangest of all is that the sleeves have been transposed, left to right, and visually extended. They are in fact sleeves in which the mail and plate elements reached to just above the elbow. The artist has drawn them as being full length, the circular elbow plate being positioned at the armpit.

Lot 440 of the Oxenham's sale was bought by the Armouries at the Tower of London, which was acquiring interesting items at that time to add to its collection. The actual sale and subsequent acquisition of this armour is described by Beard.[44] It was almost certainly there that the armour was reassembled, using a green worsted braid in place of the original silk. An old photograph of the Horse Armoury at the Tower, taken about 1860, shows the armour (now catalogued as XXVIA.2, figure 15) on a dummy stood in front of a pillar holding a curved sword and equipped with suitably curly toed shoes to give credence to its Moorish origins, though it is identified as Japanese in Hewitt's catalogue of the previous year.[45] Interestingly, these same curly toed shoes still exist in

---

44 C. R. Beard, 'Some Tower Armour Pedigrees', *The Connoisseur*, March (1931) 159–64.

45 J. Hewitt, *Official Catalogue of the Tower Armouries* (London, 1859), 113, no. XV.472–3

the oriental collection of the Royal Armouries. During the first part of the twentieth century the armour was confused with one of the armours given to James I. It was only recognized as the one bought in 1841 during the second half of the century.

The armour is technically a *mogami haramaki*. Armours of mogami construction have the traditional rows of scales replaced by solid plates, each plate in the dō being individually hinged in four places to allow it to be opened to put on. The sei ita, a separate narrow plate with its own *kusazuri* fastens to the dō behind the shoulders and is held in place by the waist belt. Decorating the armour are gilded copper plaques held by gilded rivets engraved with the kamon originally used by the Shimazu family of Satsuma in the form of the character for the number ten, *ju,* in a circle. By the late 1500s, most of the Shimazu had replaced the ju character by a geometric cross that joined the outer border, giving a shape similar to the cheek piece of a horse bit. It is said that the reason for this change was to avoid the confusion with a Christian cross. Indeed, for quite a time in the 1960s and 1970s the armour was thought to have belonged to Naito Yukiyasu, a Christian daimyō exiled to Manilla because the kamon does indeed look like a Christian cross in a circle. However, a close examination of these rivets shows the presence of a small upward tick at the base of the upright showing it is in fact the character ju.

During conservation a fragment of original black lacing survived trapped between two plates confirming that this armour is none other than that described in the 1603 order of transfer from the Treasure House to the Real Armería in Madrid. The helmet also corresponds in that it is described in the movement order as having a gilded leather panache or crest and in front a crest with a cross; the Shimazu kamon. Although these crests were lost long ago, the helmet has two large prongs on top for the gilded crest and another on the brow. Also described in the document are the gilded copper plaques fastened in place by gilded copper rivets decorated with the same kamon. There are four on the *dō* and one survives on the hand guard, exactly as described in the document.

In summary, we have seen that there remains around Europe a number of early Japanese armours which once belonged to people who played very important roles in the unification of Japan. The remains of three, now very badly burned, are in the Real Armería, Madrid, four are in the Musée de l'Armée, Paris, two are in Schloss Ambras, Austria, two are in the Royal Danish Kunstkammer, Copenhagen and three are in the Royal Armouries in England. There was one complete armour in the Reale Armeria in Turin in the late nineteenth century, together with parts of another, now reduced to one helmet.

Several other armours known to have been in Europe are now lost. One of the armours given to the Dutch is missing, as is that depicted in the painting of Sir Neil O'Neill, although they may be one and the same. There is no evidence of the fate of the armour given to Saris by

Matsuura Hōin, or to that given to Cocks unless the latter is that in the Wright painting. Assuming that the armours in Copenhagen are those originally given to the Medici, there is also the mystery of the red-laced armour described as having a hair covered helmet that was in Madrid. It is almost certainly one of the three that went to Gadalajara and was subsequently sold in Paris but its present whereabouts is unknown. One of the Royal Armouries armours almost certainly belonged to Takeda Katsuyori. Another was the property of a member of Shimazu family in the 1560s or 1570s. One of the armours in Austria and one in Madrid belonged to Hideyoshi prior to his appointment as regent. Two of those in Paris and one in Madrid belonged to him after his elevation to regent. Unfortunately, Japanese heraldry is not as precise as that used in Europe and it has not been possible to positively identify the original owners of the other armours. It is hoped that this situation might change as more information becomes available.[46]

---

46 I would like to thank Dr Thom Richardson for providing extra detail and help with the references.

The Horned Helmet of Henry VIII: A Famous Enigma

Graeme Rimer
Curator emeritus

This helmet (figure 1) was the subject of an acrimonious debate between two eminent armour scholars which was published in 1974.[1] The eminence of the protagonists, and the vehemence with which the views they held were exchanged, overshadowed this piece since that time, and few other students of arms and armour were willing to enter the fray.

In 2009 the Royal Armouries held a major exhibition to mark the 500th anniversary of the accession of Henry VIII, however, and it seemed appropriate to re-examine the subject. This paper offers a new interpretation of this remarkable object and the result of research he undertaken during the past three decades or so.

This helmet owes its survival to its uniquely odd appearance – its ugly face, its spectacles and its extraordinary horns make it an unmistakeable object. The rest of the armour to which it originally belonged was apparently sold off as scrap metal at the end of the English Civil Wars in 1649, but the strange appearance of this helmet must have helped to preserve it from destruction. Indeed its unique nature is so great that it led to it becoming the symbol to represent the new Royal Armouries Museum when it was opened in Leeds in 1996, and is now the image on all directional signs helping visitors find their way there (figure 2).

This study of the Horned Helmet begins with an important article

---

[1] A. Borg, 'The Ram's Horn Helmet', *Journal of the Arms & Armour Society*, VIII.2 (December 1974), 127–37, and C. Blair, 'Comments on Dr Borg's "Horned Helmet",' ibid., 138–85.

Figure 1 The famous horned helmet of Henry VIII, Innsbruck, 1511–14 (Royal Armouries IV.22)

by the great arms and armour scholar, Claude Blair, then Keeper of Metalwork at the Victoria and Albert Museum, published in *Archaeologia* in 1965.[2] Sadly since the author's original lecture was first prepared Blair has died, so it will now not be possible to discover his feelings about the theories proposed in the present article.

Blair's subject was the armour shown in figure 3, the Silvered and Engraved armour of Henry VIII, and he examined it in precise detail as an armour traditionally believed to have been one given to Henry by the Emperor Maximilian.

The study of armour and historical weapons had been taken up with great enthusiasm in the early nineteenth century, and the mass displays, which had existed within the Tower of London were given new life and focus. Early students of armour knew that Henry VIII had received the gift of an armour from the Emperor Maximilian I, and many believed this was that armour. Blair, however, successfully demonstrated that this was made for Henry at his own court armour workshop, established by him at Greenwich Palace very early in his reign. Blair also stated convincingly that just one fragment of Maximilian's gift armour survived – the Horned Helmet – part of a fabulous armour, now otherwise lost,

Figure 2 Royal Armouries street sign with Horned Helmet logo (Royal Armouries)

---

2 C. Blair, 'The Silvered Armour of Henry VIII in the Tower of London', *Archaeologia* XCIX, (reprinted 1965).

which had originally been decorated with pierced and gilded silver panels.

In 1974 Blair's analysis was questioned by Alan Borg, at that time Keeper of Edged Weapons of the Royal Armouries at the Tower of London in his article in the *Journal of the Arms and Armour Society*. He began with the first description of the gift armour, from the 1547 Inventory of the effects of Henry VIII:

> Item; upon a third horse a harness given unto the kings Majesty by the Emperor Maximilian, with a base [i.e. skirt] of steel and goldsmith work, silver and gilt with a border about the same - silver and gilt of goldsmith's work - and a bard [horse armour] of steel with a Burgundian cross and the fusye [fire-steel] and a saddle with a crymmyn [crinet, neck defence] and shaffron to the same.

Borg noted Blair's view that this could not be the Silvered and Engraved armour, since this was listed elsewhere, described thus:

> ffirst A complete harness with a long base all over engraven and parcel gilt with roses and pomegranates which was king Henry the VII th his harness

The association given of this armour to Henry VII rather than Henry VIII is now regarded as a scribal error. The third significant entry is this:

> Item vpon a third horse a plain tilt harness lacking a pair of gauntlets, a base cote of black velvet embroidered with cloth of gold, a head piece with a ram's horn silver parcel gilt and a steel saddle covered with black velvet.

This suggests that the helmet (the 'head piece'), had become separated from its armour. But by 1561, in an inventory made during the reign of Queen Elizabeth I, the helmet and its armour seem to have been reunited:

> Armour sent to your Majesties said father by Maximilian the Emperor garnished with silver and gilt with a Headpiece of fashion like a Ram's head.

Figure 4 Engraving of William Sommers's armour by L (or I) Herbert, London, 1794 (Royal Armouries)

The next inventory, of 1562, listed the armour sent to Henry by Maximilian but did not mention the Horned Helmet.

A Tower inventory of 1611 listed the helmet separately and by 1638 it was shown as part of the armour said to be that of Henry VIII's fool, Will Sommers. After the Restoration of Charles II in 1660, when the Tower was becoming more overtly a show place celebrating Britain's monarchy and military might, it remained identified as Will Sommers' armour, and continued to be so until the mid-nineteenth century. It is shown in an eighteenth-century engraving (figure 4):

Borg challenged the documentary evidence put forward by Blair in support of the proposal that the Horned Helmet was indeed part of Maximilian's gift armour. Despite an inventory description of 1660, which described an:

> Antique headpiece with Ramshorns, Collar, and spectacles upon it, one jack [i.e. body defence], and one sword, all said to be William Sommers arms

Borg suggested that the mask might not have been present. He

Figure 5   Armour made for Charles V as a youth by Konrad Seusenhofer, Innsbruck, about 1512, with detail of the skirt (Hofjagd- und Rüstkammer, Vienna)

did, however, describe the form of the helmet as highly unusual. He questioned too the assertion made by Blair about contemporary documents preserved in Austria which recorded the plans of Maximilian to have three armours made as gifts. All ordered from his own master armourer, Konrad Seusenhofer, in Innsbruck, these were to be presented to George III Ilsung (a wealthy merchant of Augsburg and owner of Castle Tratzberg, Austria), Henry VIII of England, and the emperor's own grandson, the Archduke Charles, later the Emperor Charles V. The armour for George Ilsung is lost, but that of Charles survives in the imperial collections in Vienna (figure 5).

This small armour, made for Charles when he was about twelve years of age, has a skirt of steel, in imitation of the fabric version then much in fashion in male costume, and is decorated with applied pierced silver-gilt panels attached by small rivets into recessed panels.

While none of the decorative panels that probably existed on the Horned Helmet survive, there are similarities in the form of construction to suggest that they were indeed originally fitted. In the breastplate of Charles's armour is a vacant panel. This has lost its decoration, and now has empty rivet holes around the edge (figure 6) The skull of the Horned Helmet has panels of the same form (figure 7).

Borg challenged the authenticity of the helmet, first on the grounds of the presence of a central row of small square holes running over the skull, which he suggested were incompatible with the presence of a crest if horns were originally present.

Second, he felt that the horns, which are beautifully made, appear crudely attached. Third, he thought that half-hinges, found on the forward edges of the cheekpieces, required explanation since they are not used to attach the mask. Last, he questioned the suitability of the method of attaching the mask, by a small central hinge at the brow and with some form of hooked closure beneath the chin. Borg then speculated on the reason for, or meaning behind, the extraordinary helmet, and summarized briefly the formality of the relationship between Henry VIII and Maximilian, which he felt would have given few opportunities to share private jokes.

He suggested that the mask 'superficially resembles a profile portrait

Figure 6   Detail of a recess in the breastplate of the Charles V armour showing rivet holes

Figure 7   The rear of the Horned Helmet, showing a recess for a decorative panel with similar rivet holes (Royal Armouries)

*Figure 8
(left) Family
portrait of
Maximilian I
by Bernhard
Strigel, about 1515
(Kunsthistorisches
Museum, Vienna, GG
832)*

*Figure 9
(right) Portrait of
one of Maximilian's
fools (Narrenbildnis)
by Marx Reichlich,
about 1519-20
(Yale University Art
Gallery, lent by Dr
and Mrs Herbert
Schaefer)*

of Maximilian' (shown in figure 8), but said the mask was a 'far closer likeness of one of his Fools' (figure 9). It might be thought, however, that there is actually very little similarity between this image of the emperor and the mask of the Horned Helmet, and barely one between that of the fool and the mask.

Borg then discussed the horns, suggesting that their presence was 'extraordinary', in that by the fifteenth century the symbolism of horns only really implied dishonour, or the Devil. He indicated, too, the distasteful imagery of this period which was associated with the Jews, sometimes shown horned, and gave two illustrations (figures 10 and 11):[3]

In the sixteenth century, however, the most common use of horns was to imply that the wearer was a cuckold. Borg's summary was that if Maximilian had sent Henry a horned and masked helmet it must have been a very 'in' joke indeed; that despite many descriptions of Henry's appearances in public none ever recorded this helmet; that the skull, cheekpieces and mask might not belong together; that the ram's horns are finely made but crudely attached and, finally, that the present form of the helmet would have made it unsuitable for wearing

---

3   See also R. Melinkoff *The Horned Moses in Medieval Art and Thought, California Studies in the History of Art* (Oakland CA, 1970).

by a king. He said finally that in his opinion the helmet was 'highly composite'. He concluded, though, by also saying that his remarks were 'pure speculation', but that they were not intended to be frivolous. 'The only really unshakeable fact [he said] is that we do not know.'

Blair's response to Borg's article is a model of measured control, but he was clearly immensely irritated by the tone and nature of what he clearly felt was a flawed analysis. His response was in three parts: the Austrian evidence, the English evidence and the Horned Helmet, and finally, the horns.

The Austrian evidence is based on surviving documents, including a report of June 1511 by Konrad Seusenhofer, master armourer to Maximilian I, summarizing his current tasks. (Seusenhofer is shown with the young emperor in a well-known engraving, figure 12). In this report Seusenhofer mentioned that among five armours to be made was one 'For the King of England's own person – similar in every way to Ylsing's, together with the same wrought silver'. This armour was to be a gift from Maximilian to Henry. George Ilsung's armour

Figure 10 (left) Lucas Cranach's title page for Luther's 'Von den Jüden und Ihren Lügen' (The Jews and their Deceitfulness), 1543 (Bayerische Staatsbibliotek, Munich)

Figure 11 German broadside 'Der Jüden Ehrbarkeit' (The Jews' Respectability), 1571 (Bayerische Staatsbibliotek, Munich)

47

*Figure 12
Maximilian I
in Seusenhofer's
workshop, woodcut by
Hans Burgkmair from
'Der Weisskünig' (The
White King)*

*Figure 13   The horned
helmet showing the
right profile (Royal
Armouries IV.22)*

is lost, but it was ordered at the same time as one for Maximilian's grandson, the young Archduke Charles, whose armour we have already seen. All three armours were to be decorated with gilded and pierced silver panels laid over pieces of rich velvet. The documentary evidence therefore indicates the strong similarity between the armours to be made for Ilsung, Charles and Henry. Armours with overlaid panels of this kind were always very rare, so the physical similarities between the construction of the Charles V armour and the Horned Helmet must suggest a clear association.

Blair quoted the entry in the 1547 inventory of Henry's effects relating to the Maximilian gift armour as decorated with *'goldsmith's work'* (i.e. applied precious metal panels), and that the only piece surviving today in the collection of the Royal Armouries which matches is the Horned Helmet. He summarized Borg's suggestion that the recessed panels could have contained other types of decoration, but dispels this with the observation that, given the provenance of the Horned Helmet and the known historical parallels for it, this is highly unlikely. Blair argued that at least the skull should be regarded as part of the gift armour, and went on to discuss the case for the cheekpieces and the mask.

The case for the cheekpieces is that they are a precise fit with the skull, and that they are of unusual form, in not enclosing the wearer's

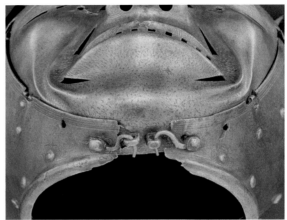

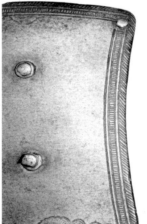

Figure 14   Armet, possibly by Konrad Seusenhofer for Henry VIII, Innsbruck, about 1510–15 (Royal Armouries V.412)

Figure 15   Underside of the chin showing fastening of Horned Helme. (Royal Armouries IV.22)

Figure 16   Detail of the edges of the cheekpieces and mask of the Horned Helmet, showing the similarity of their etched border decoration and also the position of the lining rivets (Royal Armouries IV.22)

chin. One can see an excellent contemporary example of an armet of the same date, and possibly also by Seusenhofer, in figure 14. Here the chin is safely protected by the two cheekpieces closing over it. Damage has obscured the original method of fastening the Horned Helmet's cheekpieces under the chin, but it must have been an unusual one (figure 15).

An indication that the mask must have fitted inside the cheekpieces is the way that the row of lining rivets is set back from the edge. Normally the quilted fabric linings of cheekpieces extend to the forward edge, and therefore need a row of lining rivets to secure the leather strap to which the lining would be stitched. The presence of the lining rivets so far back from the edge suggests that the linings could only have extended to this point, in order that the rear edge of the mask could be

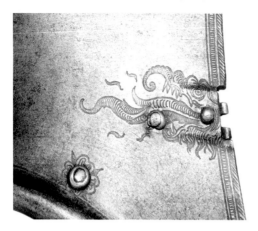

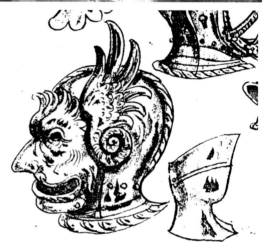

Figure 17   Etched dragon on half hinge on cheekpiece of the Horned Helmet (Royal Armouries IV.22)

Figure 18   Dragon etched on cuisse of the armour of Charles V (Hofjagd-und Rüstkammer, Vienna)

Figure 19   Detail of the page from the mid-sixteenth century 'Thun'sche Skizzenbuch', showing a grotesque helmet with detachable mask and alternative buffe

accommodated. There is also a strong similarity between the decorative etched borders of the cheekpieces and the mask (figure 16).

There is also considerable similarity between the dragon's head decorating the location of the half-hinges on the cheekpieces (figure 17), with a similar motif etched on the cuisse of the Charles V armour (figure 18), and from this evidence Blair felt that the mask must be original to the helmet.

The half hinges would also appear to indicate that an alternative form of face defence (a buffe) could have been intended to replace the grotesque mask. An example of such a helmet, with an alternative buffe to replace a grotesque visor, appears in a manuscript, the *Thun'sche Skizzenbuch*, which originally recorded armour made for the Emperor Ferdinand I, brother of Charles V, the great armourer Kolman Helmschmid, of Augsburg (figure 19).[4]

4 Recently rediscovered, now in the Museum of Decorative Arts (Uměleckoprůmyslové Museum), Prague, GK 11.572-B, see Pierre Terjanian, 'Thun-Hohenstein albums, Part I. The art of the armorer in late medieval and Renaissance Augsburg: the rediscovery of the Thun sketchbooks', *Jahrbuch des Kunsthistorischen Museums Wien* 13/14 (2013), 299–395.

In their original articles Borg and Blair discussed the great distance between the eyes of the mask – far too great to be matched by any normal (or indeed abnormal) human face. Vision, however, is possible through small apertures in the mask, and the possible identity of the face, as something extraordinary, will hopefully be revealed later in this article. Blair discussed but discounted the possibility that the mask might have been made for, or to represent, Will Sommers (following a suggestion from Borg). Its exceptional quality as a piece of decorative ironwork really makes this suggestion unsupportable and Blair discarded it.

Any association with Sommers is unlikely. He did not join Henry VIII's court until around 1525, and was still in his employment at the time of the king's death in 1547, but the only mention of the helmet in the 1547 inventory is in association with Maximilian's gift armour. If there had been any association with Sommers surely the compilers of the inventory would have known.

Later inventories of the objects contained in the Tower of London Armouries, especially from 1660 onwards, contain many wildly improbable attributions (for example, a late sixteenth-century Greenwich armour was identified as that of 'William the Conqueror'). The attribution of the Horned Helmet as that of Will Summers therefore seems to have been made no earlier than the seventeenth century.

Blair discussed the similarity of the etched decoration on the Horned Helmet to that on other known Seusenhofer/Innsbruck pieces, but could not offer an explanation for the row of mostly square rivet holes running over the crown of the skull. A possible reason for this feature will be offered later in this article.

Blair then went on to discuss the horns. He felt that they were in no way 'separate from the rest of the helmet', and contested Borg's views on the crude method of attachment to the skull, and the suitability of such a helmet to be worn by a monarch. He suggested that any differences in form or colour identified between the mask and horns and the rest of the helmet was simply that within the same workshop the skull and cheekpieces could have been made by one craftsman, the horns and mask by another. He felt that the roughness of the slots was as a result of a repair. He did not subscribe to Borg's interpretation of the significance of horns and mentioned their presence on some horse armours, but also that they are to be found on three sixteenth-century

Figure 20   Parade burgonet, north Italian, mid-sixteenth century (Armeria Reale, Turin)

helmets, one of which is the one shown in figure 20.

Blair suggested that the quality of the metalworking, and the distinction of the original owners, must have meant that, to them, wearing horns was acceptable. The author, however, feels that one should consider the difference between grotesque helmets, like this example, and the very different form of the Horned Helmet. Regarding the possible identity of the face which inspired the making of the mask Blair considered Borg's remarks, but he 'could not see that speculation on the subject serves any useful purpose'. In trying to discover the inspiration for the identity of the mask one might find this comment surprising. He did consider, however, but not very seriously, Borg's idea that the identity might have been of Maximilian's jester or indeed of Maximilian himself. Blair went on to say that in all his writings about Henry VIII's activities the chronicler Edward Hall never mentioned Henry wearing a Horned Helmet. Indeed Blair made the point that no specific contemporary descriptions of any of Henry's armours survive from before the rather brief descriptions in the Inventory of 1547.

He concluded his response by suggesting that diplomatic gifts were different to personal ones, and discounted the possibility that the gift armour with its Horned Helmet was an indication of some form of personal relationship. With this in mind, it is important to remember that while the gift armour was already being planned in 1511, only two years after Henry came to the throne, Henry and Maximilian did not meet in person until 1513, at the siege of Thérouanne. After a carefully crafted and presented rebuttal Blair said he hoped to have proved Borg's conclusions were 'without substance'.

A possible identification

This debate was published almost forty years ago, and because of the acrimony it stimulated the Horned Helmet has remained a topic few arms and armour scholars would go near for fear of provoking one or even both protagonists. For almost all that time, however, the author has had his own thoughts on this most controversial piece, and they, like Blair's, can be divided into three parts: the spectacles, the mask and the horns. First the spectacles:

There is no mention of the mask or its brass spectacles in the 1547 Inventory, only a 'head piece with a ram's horn', but they certainly were in place when the helmet formed part of 'Will Summers's Arms' in the seventeenth century. One might find it surprising that they were not discussed in the Borg–Blair debate. At times the relationship of the spectacles to the Horned Helmet has been doubted, and at times they were indeed removed and the helmet shown without them. It is remarkable that they have survived.[5]

A brief look at some contemporary images of this type of spectacles (known as 'rivet' spectacles because of the riveted joint that enables them to grip the bridge of the wearer's nose) will show that this design was common, if not ubiquitous, by the early sixteenth century (figures 21 and 22).

Figure 21 (left) Detail from 'The Virgin with Joris van der Paele' by Jan van Eyck, 1434–6, showing van der Paele holding a pair of spectacles (Groeningemuseum, Bruges)

Figure 22 (right) Detail of a copper or silversmith, or pewterer, wearing spectacles, in 'The Children of Mercury', from 'The Children of the Planets' by the Housebook Master, about 1475–85

Figure 23   Retainers dressed as fools from Marx Walther's 'Turnierbuch und Familienchronik' (Bayerische Staats-bibliotek, Munich, no. BSB Cgm 1930, pp. 12 and 13)

Despite the disinclination of Borg and Blair to explore further the possible inspiration of the identity of the mask this author believes the spectacles are an integral part of the key to the mystery and hopes to demonstrate this.

For many years I thought the face of the Horned Helmet was that of a fool. In Germany by the late fifteenth century the use of the fool as a figure to represent human failings, foibles and weaknesses was very well established, to the extent that the figure had become stereotyped and instantly recognizable. There are many hundreds of examples, of which figure 23 is but one:

The presentation of human frailty through the image of the fool is perhaps best represented by the publication in 1491 by Sebastian Brandt of *Das Narrenschiff*, or *Ship of Fools*, an extended poem in 110 chapters, each summarizing a form of human failing.[5] The book was a major success throughout Europe; originally published in 1491 in German, it was soon translated into Latin and then into many other languages. The English translation, with some additional text of his own, was by the poet and clergyman Alexander Barclay, and was published in 1509.

Each chapter begins with a woodcut, many by famous artists, including Albrecht Dürer. Among these are images which perhaps help shed light on the inspiration for the mask of the Horned Helmet (figure 24, left). Here an apparently learned figure, a bibliophile (or

---

5   The author is very grateful to Dr Thom Richardson, Deputy Master of the Royal Armouries, for first bringing Brandt's work to his attention.

bibliophool, ed.), sits in his library surrounded by books, the contents of which he confesses he does not understand. Note that he wears a fool's cap with its characteristic bells, which is thrown back, and a pair of spectacles.[6] Spherical bells play a significant role in the visual vocabulary identifying fools (figure 24, right). In this image several figures are seen in apparently learned discussion, but while they appear to be serious scholars their robes are decorated with bells, indicating foolishness, a fact confirmed in the title, 'Of Useless Studying', of this chapter of the work.

The fool became readily identified by his close-fitting hood equipped with asses ears tipped with bells, often with a row of bells or a cocks-comb running over the top of his head. Another image (figure 25), shows how readily the image of the fool was understood in German lands by this

Figure 24   Left, 'Of Useless Books' Right, 'Of Useless Studying' from Sebastian Brandt's 'Das Narrenschiff' (1491)

---

6   A question sometimes asked about the spectacles of the Horned Helmet is whether or not they were ever fitted with glass lenses. It is clear from examining them that they were not. They were simply a feature of the character whose face inspired that of the mask.

Figure 25   The distribution of fools' caps ('Narrenkappe'), woodcut by Erhard Schön, 1538 (© Trustees of the British Museum)

Figure 26   'Woman Cutting Her Chastity Belt', an engraving by Peter Flötner (© Trustees of the British Museum)

date. The woman on the right in the cart is apparently offering a free cap-fitting service to foolish men.

By the early years of the sixteenth century many overtly crude, grotesque, or downright obscene images, many featuring fools, became increasingly popular in Germany and elsewhere. A particularly prolific artist of this genre was Peter Flötner, whose name is a play on words, a *Flettner* being a lewd old man, and it is Flötner's work which perhaps gives us the best clues to the identity of the mask of the Horned Helmet. Figure 26 shows a 'Woman Cutting Her Chastity Belt',[7] and there is a fool in typical garb kneeling to her right. Note that he is wearing spectacles.

Figure 27 shows some playing cards by Flötner, where the suit emblem is, significantly, bells. They date from the mid-1530s. Note that fools appear in

---

7   This was discussed by C. Grössinger, 'Humour and Folly in Secular and Profane Prints of Northern Europe, 1430–1540', *Studies in Medieval and Early Renaissance Art History* 35 (Turnhout, 2002). For a discussion of the work of Peter Flotner see E. F. Bange, *Peter Flotner: Meister Der Graphik* Band XIV (Leipzig, 1926). The figure of the *Schellenunter* as a bespectacled fool appears among a number of designs for playing cards on p. 20.

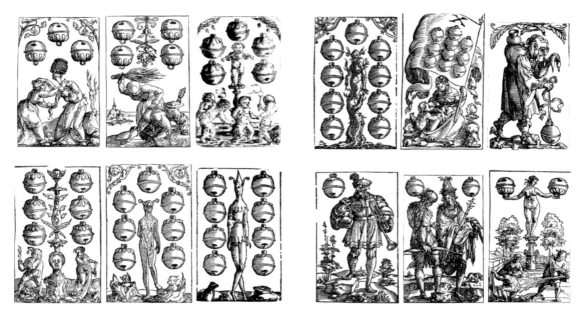

Figure 27   Designs for a suit of playing cards in bells by Peter Flötner, 1537 (Royal Armouries Library)

cards 7 and 8. The rest of this suit contains a particularly significant figure – the *Schellenunter* or Knave of Bells. This image deserves closer examination (figure 31).

This figure has the distinctive hood of a fool with ears and bells and over his head is a cock's-comb. It has been made more grotesque by the hump on his back so large that it can support a pot, and by being given a deliberately obscene sausage in his hand. His facial features are of particular interest, for he wears spectacles and his large hooked nose is running copiously. The mask of the Horned Helmet as noted also has these features (something not mentioned in the earlier articles), including the dripping nose. Note that the mask of the Horned Helmet is etched with wrinkles around the eyes and a stubbly chin, features to enhance the uncouth appearance of the character upon whom it is modelled.

Figure 28   The 'Schellenunter' card representing the jack or knave (Royal Armouries Library)

57

Figure 29   The horned helmet and the head of the 'Schellenunter' shown together

Figure 30   Modern reconstruction drawing of the possible appearance of the original gift armour of Henry VIII imitating the armour of Charles V shown in figure 5 (Royal Armouries)

This could explain the row of square holes running over the skull of the helmet. They were perhaps to attach a row of individual leaves forming a cock's comb, each leaf held by a single rivet. A square hole would prevent the rivet turning and the parts of the cock's comb from becoming disarranged.

But what of the horns? While it can be accepted that the mask may have been modelled on the popular image of a fool, it is nevertheless true that none of the many hundreds of images of fools in circulation at that time is shown wearing horns. Further, it has always struck the author as odd that the horns might indeed have originally been fitted to a helmet to be worn by Henry VIII, especially given their known use to imply cuckoldry. The modern reconstruction shown in figure 33 shows the Horned Helmet in its current form fitted on to a scaled-up version of the armour made for the youthful Charles V confirms this: it looks, at best, incongruous.

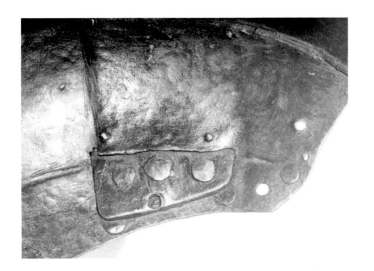

Figure 31   Interior of the Horned Helmet, showing rivets holding horn in place (Royal Armouries IV.22)

Yet the horns on the Horned Helmet are very finely made. They are hollow, formed from a flat sheet of iron, but extremely well worked to represent a pair of curled ram's horns. The outer surface shows traces of fine etched decoration, perhaps originally gilded, to give the horns the natural texture of those of a sheep. Despite Blair's views, the author's opinion is that the horns are indeed poorly fitted, especially if one considers they were made by, or at least under the direction of Konrad Seusenhofer, Maximilian's own master craftsman and one of the finest armourers then working in Europe. An interior view of the fitting of the horns may support this view (figure 31).

Note the features shown here: the crude folded-over and flattened end of the horn (apparently with its decoration incorporated into the folded end), the large crude rivets, and particularly that the end of the horn overlaps the lining strap rivets, which would have made the fitting of a lining impossible. This last feature seems to suggest that the lining must have been removed or was missing by the time the horns were fitted.

Blair mentioned where horns occur on armours and focused on the embossed horns found on three fine decorated grotesque helmets, but, if one can accept that the mask is the face of a fool, and that at the time the helmet was made no images existed of fools wearing horns, where else might one look? Perhaps to the area considered but discounted by Blair, contemporary horse armours. Several examples exist among

Figure 32 Horse armour, possibly by Kunz Lochner, Nuremberg, mid-sixteenth century, shown here in the Museo del Ejército in the 1960s, while it was still in Madrid, before its move to Toledo (Royal Armouries)

mid-sixteenth-century horse armours made in Germany, especially it seems by Kunz Lochner (figures 32, 33 and 34).[8] A similar armour is in the Kremlin Museums, Moscow, but unfortunately no image of it could be obtained. These are all carefully worked free-standing horns, resembling stylized ram's horns, for dramatic effect in parades, but there is one more example more closely related to the Horned Helmet's horns than these. This image appears in the *Inventario Illuminado*, the manuscript made around 1520 by the great armourer Kolman Helmschmid, to record the arms and armour of the Charles V. The original armour, however also survives in the Real Armería in Madrid (figure 35).

---

8 There is an historic link between the armourers of the Lochner family and Henry VIII. It seems that Kunz Lochner, the father of the maker of these horse armours, was one of the Almains, German armourers working for Henry VIII by 1515 in his newly established court armour workshop at Greenwich Palace. See T. Richardson 'The Royal Armour Workshops at Greenwich', in G. Rimer, T. Richardson and J. P. D. Cooper (eds) *Henry VIII: Arms and the Man 1509–2009* (Leeds, 2009), 148–54. An image exists in a German manuscript of another armourer called Lochner, Ulrich Lochner, probably the brother of Kunz Lochner the younger, is shown in the Nuremberg *Hausbuch* of 1535, making a helmet in his workshop. (Stadtbibliothek Nuremberg Mendel I, Amb.317.2 f .155r). This image appears as Fig.12 in T. Richardson, 'Armourer's Tools in England', *Arms & Armour* 9.1 (2012), 25–39.

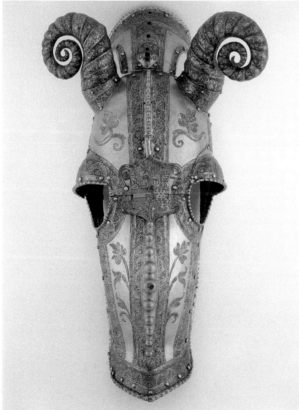

Figure 33   Lochner's armour for Sigismund II Augustus of Poland, Nuremberg, about 1550 (left) and a detail of the horns on the shaffron (Livrustkammaren, Stockholm)

Figure 34   The shaffron for Lochner's horse armour, probably for Philip II of Spain, Nuremberg, before 1567 (Real Armería, Madrid A243, Patrimonio Nacional)

Figure 35   Horse armour from the 'Valladolid' garniture of Charles V, by Kolman Helmschmid, Augsburg, about 1520, illustrated in the 'Inventario Illuminado' (Real Armería, Madrid, Patrimonio Nacional)

Below, the shaffron with horns removed, the horns detached and a front view of it with them attached (Real Armería, Madrid, Patrimonio Nacional)

This is the shaffron of the horse armour, showing embossed tassels which are a feature of its decoration.

The ram's horns, which appear in the *Inventario*, are detachable, the base area of each horn made wider in order that it might be secured to the shaffron by turning-pins. When attached, these horns bear a striking resemblance to those of the Horned Helmet.

These realistically modelled and decorated horns are the closest in form and date, and indeed through Charles V, association, with those on the Horned Helmet. Is it possible, therefore, that the horse armour given to Henry by Maximilian, or indeed another that he bought from Seusenhofer (since we know Henry ordered at least two more armours), had similar detachable horns?

There is no record of the details of the form, decoration or any special features of the armours owned by Henry VIII during his lifetime. The earliest record we have is the inventory of 1547, in which the entries are fascinating but frustratingly imprecise and brief.

The Horned Helmet therefore remains an enigma. It was almost certainly originally part of the fabulously decorated gift armour from Maximilian, but the placing of the order for the gift significantly pre-dates the first personal meeting of Henry and Maximilian, so there is little likelihood of them having developed a private joke to which this helmet might relate.

It seems not to have had any association with Will Sommers. He did not join Henry's court until around 1525, and it has been argued successfully by Blair that the mask is too much a tour de force of the armourer's art to have been made to be worn by a fool.

The half-hinges on the cheekpieces show that an alternative form of face defence could be fitted to replace the mask (although the ability to make a strongly defensive helmet with cheekpieces which did not cover the chin is hard to understand). This is perhaps another argument for the horns not being fitted originally. The helmet, with a more conventional face defence but still equipped with large horns, would have been a strange thing indeed.

The purpose of this article has been to suggest that the face of this helmet is that of the fool, a type of character popularly being illustrated, published and discussed throughout Europe by the early sixteenth century and one which was seen to relate to the failings and frailties of all men, however grand or humble. Perhaps, therefore, this part of Maximilian's lavish gift was simply to follow the then fashionable trend encapsulated in Brandt's *Ship of Fools* and remind the new young king Henry VIII how foolish even elevated individuals could be.

All we can say with any degree of certainty is that by the time of Henry's death a helmet decorated with ram's horns was part of one of his armours preserved at his palace at Greenwich, that this is almost certainly that helmet and that by that time it had been in his armoury for over thirty years. The rest, whether or not it was ever worn or indeed if it was kept and further embellished with horns simply as a splendid curiosity, can still only be speculation. The author hopes, however, that his suggestion has proposed something new to consider about the nature and inspiration for the creation of this unique, remarkable and iconic helmet.

Acknowledgements

My sincere thanks go to several of my colleagues at the Royal Armouries, in particular Dr Thom Richardson, Deputy Master, and Karen Watts, Senior Curator of Armour and Art, for their invaluable advice on my ideas about the nature and identity of the Horned Helmet. I should also like to thank the Tudor historian Professor Tim Thornton, Pro-Vice Chancellor of Teaching and Learning at the University of Huddersfield, for the opportunity to discuss my ideas with him.

As usual in such endeavours, however, all errors, omissions and misjudgements are the author's alone.

Gifts of Arms from the Stuart Court to Spain, Russia and Japan

Guy Wilson, former Master of the Armouries

This paper is not an in-depth analysis of the arms and armour that formed part of the gifts of the Stuart monarchy to the rulers of Spain and Russia. That work has been done already by William Reid, James Lavin, Howard Blackmore, Elena Yablonskaya and others and I have little new to offer on their research.[1] Rather the aim is to put such gifts of arms into context, examining Tudor as well as Stuart practice and including a brief discussion of early seventeenth-century British gifts to Japan.

The giving and receiving of gifts has always been important to rulers and, because of their significance in the activities of warfare and hunting that were of such consequence to most rulers, arms and armour have often been included in royal gifts. However, it is also necessary to recognize that the significance of arms and armour in gift giving can be over-emphasized, that many royal gifts involved no arms or armour whatsoever, and that in many others they were but minor elements. For instance, the presents given to Queen Elizabeth I by her subjects included money, plate, jewels, foodstuffs, livestock, hawks and hounds, clothing and books.[2] Put into this context the occasional New Year's

---

1 W. Reid, 'The Present of Spain', *The Connoisseur* (August 1960), 21–6; J. D. Lavin, 'The Gift of James I to Felippe III of Spain', *Journal of the Arms and Armour Society*, XIV.2 (1992), 64–88 H. L. Blackmore, 'New Light on the "Present of Spain"', *Park Lane Arms Fair*, 22 Feb. (1998), 28–34; E. Yablonskaya, 'Seventeenth-century English Firearms in the Kremlin', in O. Dmitrieva and N. Abramova (eds), *Britannia & Muscovy: English Silver at the Court of the Tsars* (New Haven and London, 2006), 134–43.

2 F. Heal, 'Giving and Receiving on Royal Progress', in J. E. Archer, E. Goldring and S. Knight (eds), *The Progresses, Pageants & Entertainments of Queen Elizabeth I* (Oxford, 2007), *passim*.

gift to her from one of her crossbow- or gunmakers of a crossbow may seem only of minor significance, but, put into the context of gifts of hawks, hounds and other hunting equipment it takes on, as we shall see, a broader importance.[3] Like all monarchs Elizabeth frequently gave gifts in return, or, indeed, might initiate an exchange, and she used the same broad palette of material presents as her subjects gave to her and, in addition, the gifts of preferment and honours. There were, of course, reasons for the choice of appropriate gifts, whether to or by a monarch – known predilections were significant guides that helped personalize an offering, but most choices were probably governed by conventions of honour and meaning, some of which we now only partly understand. Gift-giving and politics were never far apart where rulers were concerned. From the Middle Ages to the nineteenth century at Christmas popes would bless a sword and present it to a ruler or commander deemed a 'defender of the faith'.[4] At the same time, however, he also presented them with an ornate hat and, of even greater antiquity, was the papal tradition of presenting golden roses, symbolic of Christ's majesty. While this may seem quaint and peculiar there were solid, practical reasons for such presentations. The recipients were frequently chosen with secular political considerations to the fore in order to secure alliances and to ensure support for papal policies.[5] The giving and receiving of gifts was also an important mark of a monarch's liberality and honourable status. Monarchs might give gifts to other rulers to cement a new friendship, to reinforce an old alliance, to secure trade or to bury an old grievance, and this had been going on for a very long time. There are many examples, but one quote from the Bible will suffice to illustrate this: Psalm 72 is about King Solomon. Verse 10 reads 'The kings of Tarshish and the isles shall bring presents: the kings of Sheba and Seba shall offer gifts.' There is, of course, great debate about when the Psalms were written; some time, it seems, between the eleventh and fifth centuries BC, but it shows that gift-giving between monarchs was a very long tradition. For just as long presents were given by monarchs to foreigners or vassals to reinforce

---

3 G. Wilson, 'From Bolt to Ball: English Crossbows in the Tudor and Stuart Periods', *Park Lane Arms Fair*, Spring (2009), 65.

4 C. Burns, 'Papal Gifts to Scottish Monarchs: The Golden Rose and the Blessed Sword', *Innes Review*, (1969), 180; F. Warmington, 'The Ceremony of the Armed Man: The Sword, the Altar, and the *L'homme armé* Mass', in P. Higgins (ed.) *Antoine Busnoys: Method, Meaning and Context in Late Medieval Music* (Oxford, 1999), 99–102.

5 Warmington (1999), 109–15, 123–7.

their loyalty and to thank them for some service either successfully completed or about to be undertaken. And, of course, presents were also given to monarchs by their subjects and those desiring their favour to mark an important event in their life or as tokens of loyalty and respect or, sometimes, in apology for past errors.

For nearly a century anthropologists and sociologists have been analysing the whole phenomenon of gift-giving. It was the Frenchman Marcel Mauss (1872–1950) who first really brought this area of study to the attention of more than specialist scholars. In 1925 he published case studies of Melanesia, Polynesia and north-western North America and analyses of evidence from early Classical, Indian and Germanic sources to demonstrate that the exchange of gifts is a system at the centre of many if not all societies that creates a bond of obligation between the giver and the receiver that must, eventually, be reciprocated if social position, reputation or honour, call it what you will, is to be maintained. Since then his ideas have been taken forward by many others. His book, *The Gift*, was first published in English in 1954 and, although not without some critics, his ideas have been espoused by numbers of British and American historians, but not, so far, it seems by scholars of arms and armour.[6] His ideas are useful in many ways and throw light on to otherwise apparently quaint survivals like royal gift-giving. In the field of arms and armour, for instance, they considerably strengthen the widely suggested but uncorroborated idea that a major reason for the establishment by King Henry VIII of royal armour workshops at Greenwich was his need to compete in the gift exchange of armours then prevalent between European monarchs.

The royal, diplomatic and trade gifts to Spain, Russia and Japan that form the subject of this paper can be seen as very different examples of gift exchanges. In the case of Spain, diplomacy was to the fore, though with a clear intent to improve the lot of British traders. In the case of Russia, diplomacy and trade were more equally matched and the royal court and the Muscovy Company were both equally involved. Whereas with Japan trade was paramount, royal involvement was tangential and the East India Company took the major and critical decisions. What, if any, difference this made we shall now explore.

---

6 M. Mauss, *The Gift: Forms and Functions of Exchange in Archaic Societies* (London and Glencoe IL, 1954), *passim*.

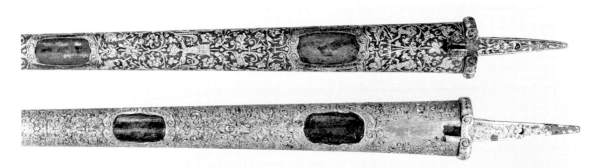

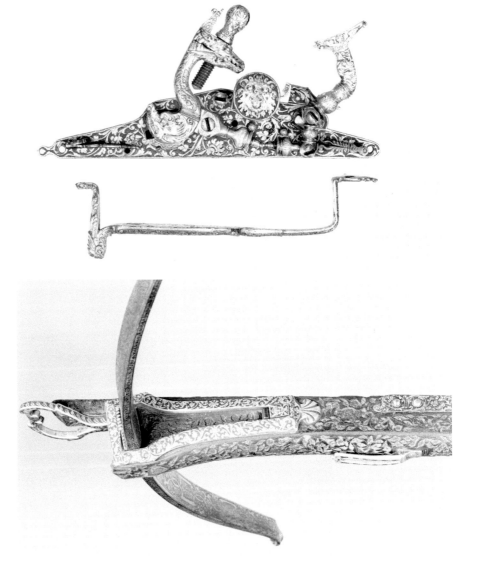

Figure 1   Surviving elements of the 1604 gift to Spain, now in the Real Armería, Madrid. Top, fowling piece barrels by John Cradocke, Real Armería K127, K129; centre, snaphance lock by John Cradocke, Real Armería K 128; below, crossbow by John Cradocke, Real Armería J109 (Patrimonio Nacional)

In 1604 Philip III, king of Spain, received from King James VI and I a gift consisting of six fully equipped horses (three for the king, three for the queen), two crossbows, four richly ornamented fowling pieces and two, apparently exceptional, lymehounds, the special dogs that detected the quarry on the morning of a deer hunt.[7] Then ten years later Philip received another, even larger, gift from James consisting this time of four fowling pieces, six crossbows, six riding trunks (presumably some sort of case or chest), four pictures of the British royal family, thirty-nine hunting dogs of five different types, sixteen horses (eight of them amblers and two with decorative caparisons), two cormorants, two pied rabbits and two pied bulls.[8] The survival in the Spanish Real Armería of numbers of the generally beautifully decorated guns and crossbows from these gifts (see figure 1) has perhaps misled us into thinking that they were primarily made up of arms and armour, but clearly they were not. They are gifts that overwhelmingly consisted of animals, weapons and accessories to be used when hunting. To the significance of this we shall return, but for now it is enough to recognize the nature of the gift. Both from the surviving examples and from the contemporary descriptions it is also clear that all elements of the gifts were of the highest quality. The maker or makers of the guns and swords for the earlier gift have not yet been positively identified. Howard Blackmore, however, has shown conclusively that the guns and crossbows of the later gift were supplied by the London sword cutler John Cradocke, and has surmised that he would have ordered them from specialist craftsmen and then would, himself, have added the fine false damascened and inlaid decoration to them.[9] James Lavin, on the other hand, follows Claude Blair in suggesting that the decoration on at least one of the guns and one of the crossbows of the earlier gift was done by decorators who were also working for the London cutlers Nathaniel Matthew and Robert South, the latter serving both James I and Charles I as a royal cutler.[10] Whoever made them, the guns and crossbows were the best that Britain could produce and so, we may surmise, were the animals

---

7   J. Cummins, *The Hound and the Hawk: The Art of Medieval Hunting* (London, 1988), 22.

8   Lavin (1992), 64–5.

9   Blackmore (1998), 31–2.

10 J. F. Hayward, 'English Swords 1600–50,' in *Arms and Armor Annual*, vol. 1, ed. R. Held (Northfield IL, 1973), 156; C. Blair, 'An English Sword with an Ottoman Blade in the Swiss National Museum – The Hilt and Scabbard' in A. Meyer and E. E. Zehnder (eds), *Blankwaffen: Festschrift Hugo Schneider zu seinen 65. Geburtstag*, Zurich 1982, 63; Lavin (1992), 80–1.

that went to Spain with them. So, what inspired this lavish gift from monarch to monarch?

When James VI of Scotland, son of Mary Queen of Scots, became king of England as James I in 1603, England, but not Scotland, had been at war with Spain for some eighteen years and, although the conflict had been intermittent, it had been costly. James, who had feared Spanish attempts to interfere with his succession until he actually reached English soil, determined on peace. The French under King Henry IV had made peace with Spain in 1598 leaving England and the Netherlands to soldier on alone. The burden was too great, and soon after his accession James put the case bluntly to de Rosny, the French ambassador, 'How can you expect me to live at war in order that you may live in peace?'[11] In addition James disliked the Dutch, whom he saw, as, of course, did the Spanish, as rebels against their king.[12] In fact both sides were ready for a fresh start. Philip III, who had come to the throne in 1596, had inherited the war with England from his father and had found his treasury empty as a result. As a result of this mutual desire for an end to the war, a peace conference was held at Somerset House in the summer of 1604. The Habsburg delegation numbered six, three representing Spain and three the Spanish Netherlands. The British delegation was only five strong and consisted of James's Secretary of State Robert Cecil, the Lord Treasurer Thomas Sackville, 1st Earl of Dorset, Charles Blunt, 1st Earl of Devonshire, and two members of the Howard family, Henry, 1st Earl of Northampton, Lord Warden of the Cinque Ports and Charles, 1st Earl of Nottingham, Lord High Admiral. The Habsburgs, while wanting a lasting peace were suspicious, especially of Cecil and of Northampton who was firmly in Cecil's camp, and they had reason to fear Nottingham, too, who as Lord Howard of Effingham had proved such a doughty opponent in 1588. Nevertheless good will and common sense prevailed and a peace treaty, the Treaty of London, was agreed that was to remain in force until 1625. Essentially this treaty restored the situation to what it was before the war had begun. On the one side Spain gave up its attempt to restore the Catholic faith in England and allowed English merchants full liberty of trade and

---

11 A. J. Loomie, 'Sir Robert Cecil and the Spanish Embassy', *Bulletin of the Institute of Historical Research* 42 (1969): 30.

12 G. Davies, *The Early Stuarts 1603–1660* (Oxford, 1959), 49.

freedom from molestation in Spanish possessions in Europe, but not overseas.[13] On the other side England agreed to cease its support for the Dutch rebels, stop the disruption of Spanish trade and colonization and open the English Channel to Spanish shipping. The treaty, signed in London in August 1604 and ratified finally by Spain in Valladollid in 1605,[14] was and is widely regarded as being the best deal possible for both sides and a triumph of diplomacy, but Cecil's inability to wring complete free trade concessions from the Spanish created enduring tensions and there was a considerable segment of British society who considered continuing war with Spain to be a better option. Indeed the peace was denounced from many more than one pulpit.[15]

The negotiation and signing of the Treaty of London had been accompanied by magnificent celebrations that were dictated by the prevalent etiquette of European court life, and amid the audiences, banquets and ceremonies there were also lavish exchanges of gifts.[16] Even after the peace was ratified, the Spanish continued to be suspicious of English intentions and especially those of Robert Cecil. To keep him as much on their side as was possible, and in line with contemporary custom, they had begun to pay him a pension during the negotiations and continued to do so and to lavish him with gifts thereafter as well as making payments to some members of his 'party' – all on the grounds that 'he has not done the harm he could and was supposed to do' and 'it keeps that man from doing all the mischief that he wants'.[17] These bribes, as we would call them today, together with the lavish entertainment and gift giving, cost Spain dear. But as Don Pedro de Zúñiga, the Spanish ambassador, once reminded his king, to stay in London without money to distribute was 'to preach in the wilderness'. In fact, for all this Spanish concern about his motives, Cecil seems to have been sincere. Despite also receiving pensions from the Dutch and the French and despite frequent tensions with Spain over trade, the treatment of English Catholics, Dutch and French manoeuvrings and English attitudes towards the pope, James's Secretary of State remained

---

13 Ibid.: 50.
14 Loomie (1969), 32.
15 G. M. Trevelyan, *England Under the Stuarts* (London, 1965, limp edn), 108; Davies 1959: 50.
16 G. Ungerer, 'The Spanish and English Chronicles in King James's and Sir George Buc's Dossiers on the Anglo-Spanish Peace Negotiations', *Huntington Library Quarterly* 61.3–4 (1998): 310.
17 These and following details are from Loomie (1969), 31, 32, 34–5, 37, 39, 44, 51–7.

faithful to the peace accord. Indeed, as the Dutch and French moved closer together from 1606 on, Cecil worked even harder to ensure a positive relationship between Britain and Spain. Then in May 1612 Cecil died, and it soon became obvious that the condition of English Catholics was worsening without him. In the same year James joined the Protestant Union, formed in the Holy Roman Empire in 1608 and the following year agreed to the marriage of his daughter Elizabeth to Frederick, the Elector Palatine and champion of Calvinism in German lands.[18] All this increased pressure on the peace accord with Spain. However, in 1614 a new Spanish ambassador arrived in London, Diego Sarmiento de Acuña, from 1617 Count of Gondomar. Not only was he a very clever man and a brilliant diplomat but he came with an offer of marriage between James's son, Charles Prince of Wales, and the Spanish Infanta Maria Anna, a match that would be accompanied by something of which James was very much in need – a dowry of £500,000. Relations with Spain improved almost immediately.

This, then, is the background to the two gifts to Spain, one in 1604 at the time of the negotiations for and the signing of the peace treaty, the other in 1614 when a series of circumstances had worsened relations between Britain and Spain but a new ambassador had brought a new chance of peace and friendship. The giving of such lavish presents by one monarch to another performed a very important function – the gifts gave honour to the giver and to the receiver. They pronounced 'We are monarchs; we are honourable; we can be trusted' and thus helped to set the right atmosphere for delicate negotiations or the start of a new relationship. As such the things that were to be given had to be selected with care in order to reinforce this message. James's two gifts to Philip III seem to have been particularly well chosen, for without being warlike, which would have been inappropriate given the long preceding years of conflict, they were very kingly. As we have seen they were largely comprised of weapons, accessories and animals used for hunting, and hunting had long been perceived as the sport of kings.

Ancient rulers, including Egyptian pharaohs such as Tutankhamun in the fourteenth-century BC and the Assyrian king Asshur-Na-Zirpal II in the ninth-century BC, were frequently depicted hunting and were probably indulging in sport, though the images that survive to us may

18 Davies (1959), 54.

Figure 2   The Assyrian king Asshur-Na-Zirpal II, 883–859 BC, hunting lions. A relief carving from the palace of Ninevah, ninth century BC, Pergamon Museum, Berlin (Author's photograph)

also have carried the message that these rulers were the feeders and brave protectors of their people.[19] Certainly it is interesting that the Assyrian king is shown hunting a lion, for one of the gods Assyria shared with its neighbour and rival Babylon was the goddess Ishtar, who, in Babylon, was often associated with images of a lion as, for instance, on the brick reliefs of King Nebuchadnezzar II's Processional Way now in the Pergamon Museum, Berlin. For millennia monarchs were brought up to enjoy hunting, and most did. It was believed to be good training for war and also to develop bravery and character.

King John I of Portugal (reigned 1385–1433) not only hunted but he also wrote a hunting manual (*Livro da Montaria*), and in it he included this passage about the relationship of the sport to the rightful status of kings:

> Kings should prize hunting highly, and ensure that it be not brought down so low as it is nowadays; for every cowherd, priest, or vile fellow seeks to be a hunter, and it is a sorry thing that it should be permitted that such lowborn folk should take part in a thing which was elevated by many good men to preserve the status of kings.[20]

Hunting, then, was an expression of the dignity and status of kings. The gift of hunting equipment and animals by James to Philip was

---

19 H. Blackmore *Hunting Weapons* (London, 1971), 1.
20 Cummins (1988), 247.

an important statement of intent. James was saying that he was a real king and that he recognized Philip as a real king. Real kings were people of their word. The giving and accepting of these gifts helped to establish their mutual obligation as kings to make the new peace work. These were also gifts very appropriate and personal to James who was a fanatical hunter and loved most of all following his hounds as they chased a hare to exhaustion.[21] It was even reported in the first year of his reign by one of his supporters that 'sometimes he comes to council, but most time he spends in the fields and parks and chases, chasing away idleness by violent exercise and early rising'.[22] Like all monarchs he had been trained and educated to like hunting and was painted as a boy of about eight with what appears to be a sparrowhawk on his arm by the Netherlandish artist Arnold Bronckorst (active 1565/6–83).[23] Of course, because hunting was seen to be kingly and honourable as well as enjoyable, the wealthy and the noble also hunted and spent much time and money in developing and preserving great hunting estates and dynastic hunting rights. In a recent study of the violent conflicts in English royal hunting forests in the years just preceding the civil wars of the 1640s Professor Daniel Beaver has shown how embedded in early seventeenth-century English society was the symbolic power and prestige of hunting, how important to status was both the gift of the ability to hunt and the gift of venison that followed from a hunt. In Stuart times these were not just quaint old ideas but spurs to ambition and both to legal action in the courts to defend hunting rights and to the illegal imposition of wanted rights by force on the ground. They were major drivers of social interaction.[24] Seen in this context James's gifts to Spain take on a greater significance still, as something very close not only to the beating heart of the monarch but to the polity of his kingdom. The profound cultural importance of hunting was something, of course, in which Spain shared. In August 1608 the Spanish ambassador Pedro

---

21 Blackmore (1971), 155, 201.

22 J. Nichols *The Progresses, Processions, and Magnificent Festivities, of King James the First* 1828, I: 188.

23 National Portrait Gallery of Scotland no. PG 992; it was the basis for a full-length portrait of the young prince with a larger hawk painted by the English artist Rowland Lockey (about 1565–1616) now in the collection of the National Trust at Hardwick Hall, Derbyshire (inv. no. 1129115).

24 D. C. Beaver, *Hunting and the Politics of Violence before the English Civil War* (Cambridge, 2008) *passim*.

de Zúñiga wrote to Philip III giving his views on the effect of a recent gift of money to Robert Cecil: 'From what I know at present all this money has succeeded in hooding this little man, so that he acts with less hostile intent in every way.'[25] For 'hooding' he used the word *capiroteado* which is a term used in falconry. Even when describing a gift of money he was drawn to use hunting language to explain how a wild thing like Cecil could be manned or controlled.

Regarding the gifts to Russia we are in different territory. Relations with Spain, even though they were important for trade, were seen in Tudor and Stuart times as foreign policy issues that were the sole preserve of the monarch and his government. With relations with Russia this was never quite the case as, from the English standpoint, trade was by far the most vital issue. The story began in 1553 when a ship commanded by Richard Chancellor, one of three sent by the Company of Merchant Adventurers to explore the north-west passage to Asia, was blown off course to the mouth of the northern Dvina river and Chancellor was taken to the court of Ivan the Terrible. Two years later the Muscovy Company was founded in London and it was soon granted a monopoly on tax-free trade with Russia. Into Russia went ores and English cloth while from Russia came furs and tallow, much needed tar, cordage and hemp for English ships and saltpetre for English guns. English merchants soon settled in Moscow and these were followed, especially from the second decade of the seventeenth century, by craftsmen including numbers of goldsmiths, silversmiths and gunmakers, and also by mining engineers, architects, physicians and apothecaries.[26] Indeed, in the mid-seventeenth-century Tsar Alexei Mikhailovich's personal physician was an Englishman, Samuel Collins.

Both the Russian-based merchants and the Company officials in London had a major impact on English diplomacy and foreign policy towards Russia, often defraying or part covering the costs of embassies between the countries.[27] While for England the relationship was exclusively about trade, and trade was also important to Russia,

---

25 Loomie (1969), 41.

26 Yablonskaya (2006), 140–2; O. Dmitrieva, ' "The Golden Chain of Traffic": The First Hundred years of Anglo-Russian Relations' in Dmitrieva and Abramova (2006), 30.

27 Dmitrieva (2006), 21; O. Dmitrieva, 'From Whitehall to the Kremlin: the diplomacy and political culture of the English and Russian courts' in O. Dmitrieva and T. Murdoch (eds), *Treasures of the Royal Courts: Tudors, Stuarts & the Russian Tsars* (London, 2013),14, 22.

by the 1560s Russia also wanted a strong ally against its Baltic and Scandinavian neighbours, and English reluctance put continuing strains on the relationship. However, frequent embassies, talking, diplomatic assistance and present-giving, both monarch to monarch, monarch to envoy,²⁸ whether diplomat or merchant, or English merchant to tsar, preserved the lucrative trade for English merchants for almost a century, though the monopoly on free trade was short-lived and English attempts to retrieve it were a constant irritant from the 1570s on. Gift-giving in this context was not the preserve of the monarchs alone. The Muscovy Company commissioned its own presents for the tsar, including large pieces of London silver plate, and frequently added its own gifts to those sent by the English monarch to the tsar, as did the ambassadors themselves. In 1604, for example, Sir Thomas Smith, head of the East India Company and royal ambassador, gave to the Tsarevich Fyodor Borisovich as a personal gift a cased pair of what may have been either wheellock or snaphance pistols.²⁹ And in 1613, Fabian Smith, head of the Muscovy Company, presented to Tsar Mikhail Fyodorovich a parrot, some silver plate, some cloth, and a gun and a pair of pistols. The barrels of the pistols were inlaid with gold and their stocks with mother-of-pearl, while the barrel of the gun was inlaid with both gold and silver and its stock with not only with mother-of-pearl but also ivory plaques and copper, probably wire.³⁰ The contemporary descriptions of them leave little doubt that they were typical best-quality English firearms with false-damascened barrels and elaborately inlaid stocks (see figure 3).

This is not to suggest, however, that English monarchs were not directly involved. Elizabeth I and her Stuart successors maintained a regular and frequent correspondence with their brother monarchs in Russia.³¹ And, when it came to choosing presents either for Russian ambassadors in London or to be carried to Moscow by English ambassadors they and their immediate advisers, most notably the Lord Chamberlain, the Master of the Jewel House and the Keeper of

---

28 For instance, the lavish gifts given in 1617 by Mikhail Romanov to John Merrick, agent of the Muscovy Company, who had successfully brokered a peace agreement with Sweden. They consisted of clothes, a portrait of the tsar and a richly decorated *kovsh*, a boat-shaped drinking vessel. Dmitrieva (2013), 16, 20.

29 Yablonskaya (2006), 134.

30 Ibid., 135.

31 Dmitrieva (2006) 19.

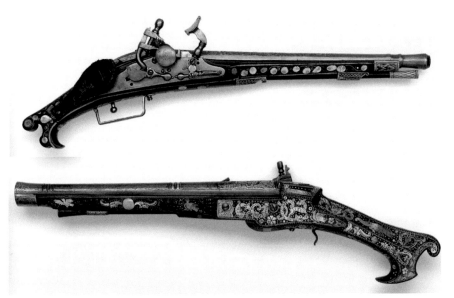

Figure 3 Snaphance pistols in the Moscow Kremlin Armoury. English pistols like that above (one of a pair, OR 3599-60 made in London in about 1617) were copied by Russian makers as can be seen from the lower pistol (one of a pair, no OR 156-7) made in the Kremlin workshops in about 1620) (Moscow Kremlin Museums)

the Privy Purse were actively involved.[32] In 1582, for instance, Fyodor Andreevich Pisemsky, on an embassy to London, was shown around the arsenal and armouries at Greenwich Palace by Sir Christopher Hatton, then Vice-Chamberlain of the Royal Household. Hatton presented Pisemsky's secretary with a sword and Pisemsky, himself, with a 'short self-shooter' from the Armoury.[33] Given the date this was probably an English wheellock pistol and may have been of the type illustrated in a portrait of Sir Martin Frobisher by Cornelius Ketel.[34] This has a recurved end to its expanding, fishtail-like butt, a feature that can be found on number of later English snaphance pistols and which clearly influenced Russian makers in the first half of the seventeenth century.[35] Whatever its precise nature the pistol given to Pisemsky was not an isolated example of the giving of arms and armour. An inventory of 1589 listing the possessions of Tsar Boris Godunov, for instance, includes an English spear and ten faceted English helmets that probably came as royal gifts.[36] However, as far as arms and armour was concerned it was English and Scottish firearms that had the greatest impact in

32 M. Jansson, 'Ambassadorial Gifts', in Dmitrieva and Abramova (2006), 203–4; Dmitrieva (2013), 26.

33 Yablonskaya (2006), 135.

34 About 1577, Bodleian Library, Oxford, no. LP 50.

35 Yablonskaya (2006), 139–140.

36 Ibid., 134.

Russia, their form and/or decoration being quite frequently copied by Russian makers.[37] Nevertheless it was elaborate English silver that was the present most frequently given to the tsars by the last of the Tudors and her Stuart successors and there is some evidence of Elizabeth's personal involvement in choosing or commissioning suitable plate.[38] Much of this silver was not newly made, and some had previously been presented to either Elizabeth or her successors by courtiers. This recirculation of gifts is by no means restricted to Britain or this period and fits well with Marcel Mauss's theories about gift exchange mentioned earlier. Some presents or intended presents were very grand indeed. It is believed that the fine portrait of Elizabeth I, known as the Hampden portrait, painted in about 1563 by either Steven van Herwijk or Steven van der Meulen, was intended to be sent to Tsar Ivan, commonly known as 'The Terrible', when a possible marriage between them was under discussion. Also, in 1604 James I presented Boris Godunov with a magnificent coach decorated with landscape paintings and carvings of hunting and battle scenes. The decoration included the theme of Christians triumphing over Turks that was clearly linked to the mission to Russia of Sir Thomas Smith who had arrived in Moscow in 1603 to discuss an alliance against the Ottoman Empire.[39] This was certainly a most kingly gift and its presentation was not an isolated incident. A coach was also given as a diplomatic gift to the rulers of Mughal India by James I in 1616 and another had been presented in 1599 by Elizabeth I to Sultan Mohammed III in Istanbul at the specific request of his wife.[40] In addition royal gifts to Russia also included hunting dogs, jewels, specie, medals, cloth, furniture, musical instruments and clocks. In return from the tsar came mostly furs and oriental textiles together with eastern arms, horses, and birds of prey for hunting with the necessary equipment. There was also an exchange of curiosities, including exotic and unusual animals and birds and the sort of lavish artworks made partly of natural materials such as coral and ivory that were popular at the time for inclusion in art collections

---

37 Ibid., 140.

38 N. Abramova, 'English Silver of the Sixteenth and Seventeenth Centuries in the Kremlin', in Dmitrieva and Abramova (2006), 36.

39 L. Kirillova, 'An English "Charyott" for Tsar Boris Godunov' in Dmitrieva and Abramova (2006), 196–7. J. Munby, "The Moscow Coach: 'A Rich Chariot One Parcell of the Great Present'" in Dmitrieva and Murdoch (2013), 159–65.

40 Munby (2013), 160–1.

and which can still be seen today in abundance in the Green Vaults in Dresden.[41] All this gift giving from monarch to monarch was part of the formalised ritual of receiving embassies at court. In Russia more than in England this ritual included parades in which the gifts were displayed to the public before they were exhibited to the court.[42] In such ways the personal gifts of one ruler to another were elevated to a status of international policy and national pride.

The lucrative trade with Russia ended abruptly with the execution of Charles I. The tsar could not forgive the 'terrible deed' of killing his 'brother' and abolishing the monarchy, so he repealed all trading privileges, banished all English merchants from Moscow and rejected the requests of both Parliament and Charles II for the resumption of trade until Charles was restored to the throne in 1660.[43] Relations between the two courts were resumed in 1662 when a Russian embassy visited London. Once more the British wanted the restoration of their lucrative trading rights, including freedom from customs duty, while the Russians wanted financial support in their war against the conjoined kingdom of Poland and Grand Duchy of Lithuania. Once more the embassy brought gifts for the king and members of his family which, apart from furs, carpets and silks included birds of prey for hunting, pelicans, martens and horses and a supply of hemp. The hemp, though not a traditional kingly gift, was directly pertinent to the negotiations as the Russian delegation promised to repay any loan with supplies of hemp and potash. Indeed this gift of hemp was even more than a guarantee of intent and goodwill. Its value represented the amount the tsar wished to borrow and was, in reality, a trade dressed up as a diplomatic gift because trading relations had not yet been formally re-established. The ploy failed and neither Charles II nor the Muscovy Company agreed to the requested loan.[44] Nevertheless the following year, Charles sent an embassy to Moscow headed by Charles Howard, 1st Earl of Carlisle, in an attempt to secure the long-desired restoration of tax-free trade. It was doomed to failure as Tsar Alexei Mikhailovich

---

41 I. Zagorodnaya, 'English Diplomats at the Court of the Tsars' in Dmitrieva and Abramova (2006), 189–92, 207.

42 Zagorodnaya (2006), 184, 187; Dmitrieva (2013), 18–20.

43 J. Hennings, "The Failed Gift: Ceremony and Gift-Giving in Anglo-Russian Relations (1662–1664)" in *International Diplomacy: Volume 1, Diplomatic Institutions*, ed. I. B. Neumann and H. Leira (London, 2013), 99–100.

44 Ibid., 91–6.

had no intention of granting this privilege and relations were further strained by disputes about protocol which, while they may appear arcane to us, were important at the time as they affected the perceived status of the respective monarchs. As a result, at the end of his mission a furious Carlisle refused to accept the tsar's presents because doing so would leave him with an obligation to the tsar. Therefore, as he explained, he could not accept until the justice he had requested on behalf of King Charles had been done.[45] It is, however, not with these spurned gifts that we are concerned but with those that Carlisle brought with him to be given to the tsar and members of his family on behalf of Charles and his queen. He also brought some personal gifts of his own but we cannot distinguish what these were from the totality of gifts listed and described. The presents included a carriage bearing gilt double-headed eagles, gold and silver plate, clocks and watches, a variety of textiles, quantities of lead and Cornish tin, six cannon and a number of guns and pistols.[46] Again it is important to recognize that guns did not make up the bulk of the gift. The present was clearly chosen in part to match and balance the tsar's gift of 1662, including the inclusion of the potential trade goods lead and tin. But the gifts were also kingly in a traditional way. At least four pieces of silver were decorated with scenes and animals of the chase, once more an allusion to the sport that bound all monarchs together in honour.[47] Others, clearly chosen by the king, himself and his closest advisers, related directly to the continuation of the Stuart dynasty after the aberration of the Commonwealth period and reinforced the request for a return to the duty-free trading status that had long been the goal of British monarchs and merchants alike. These very personal gifts included a jug and a bowl from the collection of Charles I's queen, Henrietta Maria, a gun belonging to and used by Charles I and an old pair of pistols carried by Charles II on his triumphant procession through London on this restoration in 1660.[48] Here the personal weapons of present and past Stuart monarchs were being used to carry a very clear message about the close ties between

45 G. Miege, *A Relation of Three Embassies from his Sacred Majestie Charles II to the Great Duke of Muscovie, the King of Sweden, and the King of Denmark. Performed by the Right Ho^ble the Earle of Carlisle in the Years 1663 & 1664*, (London, 1669), 305.

46 Miege (1669), 144; L. Kirillova, *The Royal Carriages: Treasures of the Armoury*, (Moscow, 2000), 25.

47 Abromava (2006), 120–7.

48 Miege (1669), 182; Henning (2013), 99–100; Zagorodnaya (2006), 192.

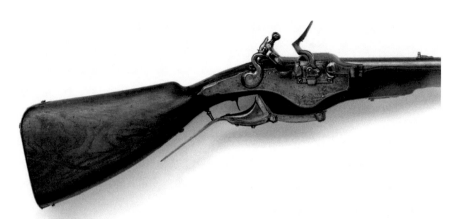

Figure 4   Flintlock magazine gun by Caspar Kalthoff, about 1658, presented to the Tsar's son, Tsarevich Fyodor Alexeivich by the Earl of Carlisle on behalf of Charles II. (Moscow Kremlin Museums OR-104)

them and their brother monarchs in Russia and about the resurgence of the dynasty.

Surviving inventories of the Kremlin, the earliest dating from 1686–87, show that Howard also brought with him two repeating magazine guns that were presented to the tsar's son, Tsarevich Fyodor Alexeivich. One can still be identified in the Kremlin's collections today (OR-104, figure 4). It was made by Caspar Kalthoff in London in 1658 and, according to an 1808 inventory, was also signed on the edge of the lockplate by Harman Barne.[49] The two men are believed to have worked together for a time so it is very possible that the inventory is correct.[50] But why should a gun, apparently made in England during the Commonwealth interregnum, form part of a Royal diplomatic gift? The answer is intriguing but space will only permit me to sketch in the outline of the story here. For details and corroborative evidence I have to refer you to my monograph on the Vauxhall Operatory.[51] Repeating magazine guns of the sort under discussion were either invented or improved by one or more of the brothers Kalthoff who came originally from the Solingen area but who dispersed around Europe to work for various monarchs. Caspar came to England and by 1634 at the latest was working at the Vauxhall Operatory (figure 5) on the site of the present headquarters of the British Secret Intelligence Service. He was employed by Edward Somerset, who became the 2nd Marquis of

---

49 Yablonskaya (2006), 164–5.

50 H. L. Blackmore, *Gunmakers of London Supplement* (Bloomfield ON, 1999), 46.

51 G. M. Wilson, *The Vauxhall Operatory: A Century of Inventions before the Scientific Revolution* (Leeds, 2009), *passim*.

Figure 5   The site of the Vauxhall Operatory from John Roque's map of 1747

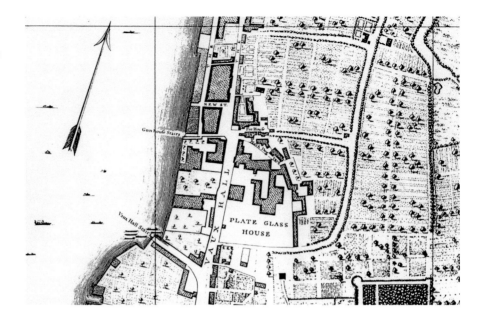

Worcester on the death of his father in 1646. Worcester, as I shall call him, was given charge of the Vauxhall Operatory by Charles I and Kalthoff was his principle engineer and model maker. The Operatory had been founded in 1629 as a secret government research establishment on principles laid out by Sir Francis Bacon. Here experiments were made on ideas and technologies that were at the edge of the possible. Some, like Kalthoff's repeating guns, underwater mines and various water-moving machines or pumps, were actually constructed, and many others were made and tested at Vauxhall in model form, including a boat that was propelled by storing and harnessing the energy of waves in much the same way as a self-winding watch works. In 1645 Kalthoff went into exile and in 1649 Worcester followed. The years of war were not good for the Operatory, but, uniquely among the king's real estate it was exempted from the sale of Charles's possessions in 1649. By 1652 Worcester had returned and was immediately imprisoned in the Tower of London. Two years later, while still in prison, Worcester managed to buy the Operatory and to get Kalthoff working there again. It was undoubtedly there that the Kremlin's magazine repeater was made. By 1663 when Carlisle set out to Moscow the Operatory was once more engaged in important work, making new types of water moving machines for use in irrigation and drainage. It is clear that Worcester and Kalthoff were the driving forces of this new inventive surge, and their work was taken seriously. An Act of Parliament was passed in 1663 allowing both Worcester and the king to profit from the invention of a new 'Water-Commanding Engine' and it seems likely that this relates to an engine independently tested and then patented in 1649 by Kalthoff while he was in exile in the Netherlands.

What more appropriate gift could there be for a future monarch, then, than a gun that was an example of the most up-to-date technology, especially when it was a technology perfected in a royal research establishment that had gone through hard times during the interregnum but was now being revived. However, there was also another very good reason for making such a gift. Kalthoff's son, also named Caspar, had, at some time before Carlisle's embassy, gone to Moscow to work for the tsar and had got stuck there. One of Carlisle's specific and personal instructions from Charles II was to bring young Kalthoff back to England[52] but in this, as in so much else, he failed. Apparently Kalthoff's period of contract had expired and when Carlisle asked for his release the tsar's chancellor seemed to grant the request. However, subsequently there was apparently a change of heart and, as Carlisle was departing from Moscow with Kalthoff in his party, the tsar sent a messenger to bring Kalthoff back to him. Carlisle did not think it right to intervene but continued to hope that the tsar would soon keep his promise and to send letters to the tsar's chancellor requesting his return even after he discovered that Kalthoff had been imprisoned instead. Subsequently it appeared that young Kalthoff had been constrained to agree to a two-year contract extension.[53] A renewed appeal for his return by Charles in 1667 after the extension had elapsed also met with failure, as, initially, did a third attempt in 1671, though there is evidence that Kalthoff was back in London by the following year.[54]

Both monarchs, it seemed, wanted the young Kalthoff badly. While Charles Howard in a diplomatic letter to the Russian Lord Chancellor, written on his journey home, emphasised the implications of Kalthoff's plight for other English craftsmen in Russia – whether in the future they were 'to be esteemed freemen or slaves' – this surely cannot be the

---

52 Miege (1669), 317.
53 Ibid., 313, 316–7, 327–8, 459–60 411.
54 Yablonskaya (2006), 142; Wilson, *The Vauxhall Operatory* (2009), 11.

Figure 6   Flintlock magazine gun made by Caspar Kalthoff the younger in the Moscow Kremlin Armoury in 1665 (Moscow Kremlin Museums OR-1947)

whole story.[55] Perhaps Charles's present of a Kalthoff repeating gun was intended to say 'You don't need the young man. We're back in business and can supply such wonders to you'. He may have been worried by the fact that both Kalthoff senior and Worcester were getting on in years and their deaths could stop the revival of the Vauxhall Operatory in its tracks unless successors could be installed. Indeed, this is just what happened, Kalthoff dying in 1664 and Worcester in 1667 while young Kalthoff, who there is reason to believe had worked with his father at Vauxhall, remained in Russia.[56] On the other hand, the tsar was obviously determined to keep hold of young Kalthoff and to get him to make such guns for him. And that, too, is what happened. In the collections of the Kremlin Armoury (OR-1947, figure 6) is a Kalthoff repeater that the young Caspar made in the Kremlin in 1665.[57] By then Caspar's father was dead and his brother-in-law was turning the site of the first British secret government research establishment into a sugar refinery.[58] By the time Kalthoff returned to England seven years later there was no chance of a revival.

We have now examined two cases of royal and other diplomatic gift giving in the late Tudor and Stuart periods within the broad confines of Europe. Finally, to make this paper just a little more relevant to the

---

55 Miege (1669), 317
56 Wilson, *The Vauxhall Operatory* (2009), 10.
57 Yablonskaya (2006), 172–3.
58 Wilson, *The Vauxhall Operatory* (2009), 50.

theme of this volume I shall compare this to what happened when relations were established between Britain and Japan at the beginning of the seventeenth century. You will find in Ian Bottomley's paper the story of these first contacts, the brief existence of an English (for so it was called) factory or trading station in Japan and the giving to James I of two Japanese armours by Tokugawa Hidetada, nominal shōgun and son of Tokugawa Ieyasu, the retired shōgun who still wielded supreme power.[59] Here I want to concentrate solely on the British attitude to gift giving in Japan at this time when the East India Company was trying very hard to establish a lucrative and lasting trade. What is striking is the lack of involvement by James in choosing the gifts to be given on his behalf. The king wrote letters to the emperor and the shōgun, but it is evident from the commission given by the East India Company to John Saris before he sailed in April 1611, that the gifts to be presented on behalf of the king were to be chosen in Japan in consultation with William Adams 'nowe resident there and in greate favour with the kinge (i.e. Hidetada)'.[60] And so they were. On his arrival in Japan Saris 'conferred with Mr. Cocks, the marchants and Mr. Addams conserning befitting presents' for the Tokugawas, their immediate advisers and senior court officials.[61] While textiles dominated all the gifts, that to Ieyasu included a gilt basin and ewer, coins, a bow, a 'prospective glass' cast in silver gilt (almost certainly a telescope) and a 'burning glass' (a mirror or lens to create fire by concentrating the rays of the sun); and that to Hidetada included a standing cup and cover. Here we can see at least some faint echoes of the types of material that were often included in royal diplomatic exchanges in Europe. To these gifts Saris added his own, again as was traditional for an 'ambassador'.[62] It was two days after giving his and the 'King's' presents to Hidetada that Adams received from him two Japanese armours for King James and two swords for himself. Although these two armours were delivered safely to the king no evidence has so far come to light to suggest that this very kingly gift

---

59 See I. Bottomley, 'Japanese Gifts of Armour to Spain in the Sixteenth Century and the Tokugawa Japanese Gift Armours to James I and the European Courts', 1–39 in this volume.
60 E. M. Satow (ed.), *The Voyage of Captain John Saris to Japan, 1613* (London: reprinted 1967 in Nendeln, Liechtenstein), xiii.
61 Ibid., 112–13.
62 Ibid., 129, 134–5.

elicited from James I a further present to continue the royal exchange of gifts and help to cement a relationship.

The predominance of textiles in these first gifts to the Tokugawas does not seem to have been the intention of the East India Company before Saris sailed. His commission, paying homage to the conventions of royal gift-giving, made it clear that he was carefully to keep for presentation to 'his Majestie or any of the noble Lords that are our honourable friends' any suitable 'faire birds or beasts, or any other rare thing fit for us to present'.[63] There is, however, no evidence that any such curiosities were presented. The Company obviously wanted to establish a good trade in textiles and instructed Saris to take special note of what sorts and colours of cloth were most popular in Japan, but he was also ordered to sell lead, iron 'and other such of our Natiue [*sic*] Comodities as by your obseruacion [*sic*] you shall finde most vendible there'.[64] In the event, over its years of trading in Japan, the Company found that textiles were the best trade goods and the apparent dominance of cloth in the initial gifts to the Tokugawas may well reflect Adams' local knowledge and his intuition that British trade in Japan must be built around textiles. Certainly subsequent gifts from the merchants of the English Factory to the rulers and nobility of Japan consisted largely of varieties of textiles.[65] Even so, however, it proved impossible to develop a really worthwhile cloth trade with Japan. Richard Cocks,[66] who was left to head the English Factory when Saris sailed home at the end of 1613, wrote to the Company in 1619 explaining the difficulties he was facing and admitted that as far as English broad cloth was concerned the Japanese did not use it much for clothing and that 'the greatest use they put it to is for cases or coverings for armours, pikes ... *cattans* ... , with muskets and guns'.[67]

In the beginning, however, it does not appear that Saris, and therefore, presumably, the East India Company, had in mind only trade involving textiles. While he was in Shizuoka meeting Tokugawa Ieyasu, before moving on the Tokyo to see Tokugawa Hidetada, he sent William

---

63 Ibid., xiv.
64 Ibid., xiii.
65 E. M. Thompson (ed.), *Diary of Richard Cocks Cape-Merchant in the English Factory in Japan 1615–1622*, 2 vols, (London, 1883, reprinted Cambridge, 2010), *passim*.
66 For biographical details of Cocks see Thompson (1883), I, xii–xvi; D. Massarella, 'James I and Japan', *Monumenta Nipponica*, 38, no. 4 (1983): 377.
67 Thompson (1883), vol. II, 311.

Adams to Ieyasu's mint master with a list of prices of commodities that were available for purchase and these included not only textiles but also tin, ivory, ordnance, sporting guns and gun powder.[68] Certainly, later Cocks and his colleagues at the English Factory sometimes included in their presents to the shōgun and other Japanese noblemen one or more English hunting guns, mostly referred to as 'fowling peeces', many said to be damascened and one to be chased.[69] The most decorated of these would have been close in form and decoration to the damascened guns given by James to Philip III of Spain and sent by successive English monarchs and merchants as presents to the rulers of Russia. On one occasion in 1615 a 'fireloct petrenell' was given, because he might be useful, to the servant of 'Calsa Samme' who seems to have been Tokugawa Yorifusa (1603–61), the eleventh and youngest son of Tokugawa Ieyasu. This gift was made six days after the same servant had made purchases for his master that included two damascened fowling pieces. Another purchase of seven damascened snaphance fowling pieces was made soon afterwards by the local lord of Firando (Hirado) where the English Factory was located. They were intended as presents to Tokugawa Ieyasu. Whether the gifts of this type of gun from Cocks and his colleagues were by then intended to promote a trade in them or whether such guns were given simply as kingly, noble and appropriate presents is uncertain, but if the English merchants hoped for major sales they were to be disappointed. The Japanese style of matchlock gun was by now irremovably embedded in Japanese life and culture. That these English guns may have been seen more as appropriate gifts rather than free trials of a sale good may be hinted at by the fact that a major gift from the English merchants to Tokugawa Ieyasu in 1616, and one more varied than many, included not only the inevitable textiles, but skins, precious materials, looking glasses, utensils, tin, lead and *Falconaria*. This gift is far more balanced than many and seems to hark back to the traditional kingly gifts of precious and unusual things, mixed with trade goods, and leavened with animals, weapons or accessories relating to hunting. The inclusion of falconry accessories was sensible and appropriate given Ieyasu's love

---

68 Satow (1900), 132.
69 These and the following details are in Cocks's diary, Thompson (1883), vol. I, 56–7, 61, 63, 65, 69, 78, 80, 84, 99, 123, 170, 175; vol II, 84.

Figure 7   English guns given as presents in Japan would have been snaphances, decorated in the same way as those included in the present of Spain and both given and sold in Russia (Moscow Kremlin Museums OR-2802)

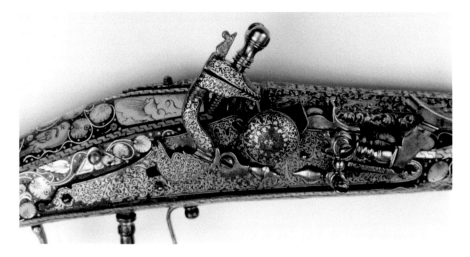

of hawking, though, like everything else they tried, it was not to lead to long-term success for the British traders.

We have seen the diplomatic gift between monarchs used as a catalyst for peace and trade, as a personal statement of restored power, and as part of a specific request for the return of a highly regarded craftsman. We have seen such gifts both succeed and fail. What is certain is that in early modern European states, despite the advent of capitalism, monarchs still valued the much older system of gift exchange that expressed their goodwill and honour and both reinforced mutual monarchical prestige and imposed mutual obligations. We do not know why James I virtually ignored the gift exchange in his dealings with the rulers of Japan and left decisions to merchants on the ground. Perhaps it was simply a sign of the relative unimportance that he and his court gave to that far-distant country and the potential for significant trade links with it. Perhaps it was due to a Eurocentric view that did not understand that gift exchange was a powerful force in the Far East, too. Perhaps it was due to a profound misunderstanding of the status of those who held power there and a lack of empathy with brother rulers so very far away. Or perhaps it was common sense to take local advice. Whatever the reason, a bond of honour and obligation was never formed by kingly gift exchange between the ruler of Britain and the ruler of Japan. Had it been, perhaps the fate of the English Factory in Japan might have been different.

A Diplomatic Gift Full of Surprises
The weapon rack of Cornelis Tromp and other 'exotic' arms belonging to Tromp and Michiel de Ruyter

Eveline Sint Nicolaas, Rijksmuseum Amsterdam

Eveline Sint Nicolaas, Rijksmuseum Amsterdam

Cornelis Tromp (figure 1) had his portrait painted twenty-two times, which is probably a record for the seventeenth century. He is reputed to have been a vain man, with a temper. By contrast, Michiel de Ruyter was far less interested in pomp and ceremony (figure 2); in fact, he once declined a gold chain offered as a gift by the viceroy of Naples. Both

Figure 1 (below left)   Cornelis Tromp (1629–91) by J. W. Munnickhuysen, after a painting by D. van der Plas, 1664–1721 (Rijksmuseum RP-P-1908-5386)

Figure 2 (below right) Michiel de Ruyter (1607–76) by H. Bary, after a painting by F. Bol, 1673-1707 (Rijksmuseum RP-P-BI-608)

Figure 3   Left, Cornelis Tromp's weapon rack (Rijksmuseum NG-NM-6087-A)

men fought on the high seas and were known on this side of the ocean as the enemy; in the Netherlands, however, they were national heroes and enjoyed unparalleled popularity.

Both Tromp and De Ruyter owned collections of non-Western weapons which are now in the possession of the Rijksmuseum, and which form the topic of this article. I propose to examine the background of these various weapons and to show how they came to

PLAAT II.

Fig 1.

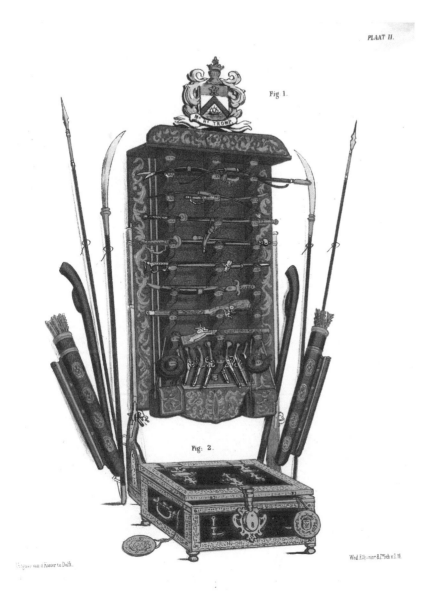

M. H. TROMP.

Fig: 2.

van 't Roever te Delft.

Wed. E.Spanier & Z.lith v.Z.M.

be owned by Tromp and De Ruyter. Were they diplomatic gifts? Were they booty or were they souvenirs, brought over from overseas voyages? And do we know anything of the role they played in the everyday lives of Tromp and De Ruyter? In this discussion, the weapon rack that belonged to Cornelis Tromp forms the central theme (figures 3 and 4).

In 1884, a year before the Rijksmuseum opened at its present location, the museum purchased a large number of weapons and an accompanying rack that had been offered by the descendants of Maarten Harpertsz Tromp (1598–1653), father of Cornelis. There were forty weapons in all, with various accessories, ranging from firearms to pole arms and edged weapons, both European and Oriental. The weapons had been offered for sale earlier, in 1819, to the Rijksmuseum's predecessor, the Koninklijk Kabinet van Zeldzaamheden (Royal Cabinet of Rarities), but lack of funds prevented the acquisition. In 1884, however, money became available, perhaps because the collection had been a star exhibit at an *Exhibition of Antiquities* held in Delft in 1863. That show was accompanied by a publication, an album containing illustrations of 'the most striking exhibits'. The weapon rack was described as follows:

> The weapon rack is made of Oriental wood, dyed red with gilt decoration. The displayed weapons, mounted on the rack and arranged around it, are mainly Oriental and were probably presented to the admiral as gifts on various occasions.

The admiral was recorded in the catalogue as Maarten Hartpertszoon Tromp, whose coat of arms surmounted the weapon rack.[1] Surprisingly, there seemed to be new information about the origin of the weapons, which were described in the catalogue as a gift from the Dey of Algiers to Tromp. The Dey had been the principal authority in Algiers as the representative of the sultan in Istanbul, although, owing to the province's distance from the Ottoman capital, he was able to exercise a considerable degree of independence. Six years later the same ensemble appeared at an exhibition of weapons, martial attributes and so forth in Amsterdam in 1869. The entire suite had been offered again for display by Tromp's descendants.

Whether the new significance of the collection played a role when the weapons were auctioned in 1884, is impossible to say.[2] Clearly the Tromp family's weapon rack and its array of weapons had made an impact on visitors to the shows, and indeed they were mentioned in various newspaper articles. At all events the timing was right and the money was available, and when the new Rijksmuseum opened in 1885, the ensemble was a part of the historical display.

---

1 *Wapenrek met verschillende wapenen zo Oostersche als anderen, geschenk van den Dey van Algiers aan den Admiraal M. H. Tromp* (Weapon rack with various weapons, Oriental and other, given by the Dey of Algiers to Admiral M. H. Tromp).
2 They were purchased at the Kasteel Maurick auction, 22 October 1884.

It was in the 1960s that questions started to be asked about the assumption that the Dey of Algiers had been the source of the gift. Tromp had certainly been active in the Levant, suppressing pirates from Algiers and Tunis on the Barbary coast who were attacking Dutch merchant ships, but there was no evidence that the Dey had given him a weapon rack.

It was also around this time that doubts were voiced at the Rijksmuseum concerning the attribution to Tromp. With his opulent lifestyle, the ensemble seemed more likely to have appealed to the vanity of his son Cornelis, although, again, no proof existed. Henceforth it was presumed that the weapons had been a gift from the Vereenigde Oost-Indische Compagnie, or VOC, the Dutch East India Company, to Cornelis Tromp. So the coat of arms of the father, Maarten, was removed from the rack, as the photograph of the display in the gallery in 1964 shows (figure 5).

Over thirty years later, when historian Ronald Prud'homme van

Reine was researching a biography of the two Tromps, father and son, he discovered confirmation in the family archive that the weapon rack had indeed belonged to Cornelis.[3] And, even more interestingly, he also uncovered the identity of the man who had given it. It was not a present from the Dey of Algiers or the VOC, but from an old friend of Cornelis Tromp living in Batavia. Thanks to the letter that this Cornelis Wemans sent with his gift on 18 March 1680, we can now trace the ensemble's origins.[4]

In 1679 Cornelis Tromp's nephew Dirk Blom was appointed to the Council of the East Indies, the Dutch company's ruling body in Batavia (present-day Jakarta), which came under direct authority of the governor general.[5] Blom had brought a portrait of his uncle to the Indies, which he gave to Wemans, who had been a friend of Tromp in his youth and who now lived and worked as a VOC merchant in Batavia. Wemans was extremely flattered to receive the portrait and noted that it was so well painted that he easily recognized his old friend, even after all those years.[6] His letter is a long panegyric singing Tromp's praises, lauding his naval successes and harking back to their youth, some forty years earlier. Wemans intended to send Tromp his own portrait in response, hoping to rekindle their connection 'and so to revive again the friendship of our youth in our latter days'. Unfortunately, that portrait would only be ready towards the end of the year and Wemans did not wish to wait to show his appreciation. So he sent him 'a local weapon rack replete with various East Indies firearms'. Wemans went on to list the weapons and items accompanying the rack.

Het geweerbort selfs root verlact en vergult.	A gun rack of red lacquer and gilt
2 patroon tasschen	2 cartridge cases

---

3 R. Prud'homme van Reine, *Schittering en schandaal: Biografie van Maerten en Cornelis Tromp* (Amsterdam, 2001), 395–6.

4 Delft municipal archive, Tromp family archive 845–54 (letter from Cornelis Wemans to Cornelis Tromp, 18 March 1680).

5 Wemens's letter states that Blom and his three children arrived in good health at Batavia on 27 July 1679.

6 '[…] *soo wel gedaan, dat ick mijner wegen onsen Jeugt en soo als ick het in ons Jongelinghschap in U excellentie gesien hadde my seer light konde herinneren*' ([…] so well done that I recalled quite clearly the antics of our younger days and how I had seen your Excellency in our youth.)

2 kruijt bussen	2 powder boxes
2 lontbussen met lont	2 fuse boxes with match
2 lodene arm ringen	2 lead arm bands
2 lodene overtrecksels	2 lead wrist guards
over de armen	
2 boogen	2 bows
2 coockers met pijlen tesamen	2 quivers with arrows in a case
in een cas	
2 musquetten met selven	2 muskets similarly mounted with
gemonteert in een kasje	cover
2 reepmessen verlackt	2 lacquered large knives
2 piecken verlackt met doppen	2 lacquered pikes with scabbards
Alle vier in lijwate holsteren	All four in linen holsters and
en met de naam van U	inscribed with your Excellency's
Excellentie geteeckent	name

In addition, Wemans included several boxes of tea for various members of the Tromp family.

Although it seems to have been Tromp who initiated this revival of contact between the one-time friends, a perusal of the letter leaves the reader with the impression that it was Wemans who felt honoured to have received the attention of the naval hero and who now saw an opportunity to improve his situation. The letter closes with a comment by Wemans expressing his uncertainty regarding a possible appointment to Ceylon (Sri Lanka). Perhaps he was hoping that his old friend Tromp might put in a good word for him back in the Netherlands.

In 1680 Tromp was living in a magnificent house on Amsterdam's Herengracht. Now in his fifties, he had married Margaretha van Raephorst, a widow, reputed by contemporaries to have been rather less than beautiful, but with plenty of money (figures 6 and 7). The house on Herengracht was hers, as was a country house on the River Vecht where the couple spent their summers. After invading French troops had ransacked and set the house ablaze in 1672, she built an impressive new edifice at her own expense, in the form of a ship. It was there, at Trompenburgh, that they kept much of their art collection (figure 8). Of an estimated 165 paintings mentioned in the estate inventory of

Figure 6   Portrait of Cornelis Tromp by Jan Mijtens, 1668 (Rijksmuseum SK-A-284)

Figure 7   Portrait of Margaretha van Raephorst by Jan Mijtens, 1668 (Rijksmuseum SK-A-285)

Figure 8   The house Trompenburgh in 's-Graveland in North Holland.

1692, around 125 were displayed at Trompenburgh, while forty were in Amsterdam.[7]

The weapon rack is described in the same inventory as an 'East Indies gun case, soot lacquered and gilded, replete with all kinds of East Indies guns, mostly inlaid with silver'. It was displayed prominently in the house in Amsterdam, in the Sael, the salon or reception room, in which the couple entertained their guests. From the inventory it seems that Tromp had added more weapons to the rack which Wemans had sent: five Dutch pistols, seven snaphances and two mother-of-pearl inlaid carbines. Evidently the gift from Batavia had provided the foundation for a display of Tromp's own collection in Amsterdam. While the pistols and snaphances were his personal weapons, the other items he added were acquisitions collected on his numerous voyages.[8] Thanks to Wemans's letter we can now distinguish which of the weapons originally belonged to the rack, and which were added to the display by Tromp and his family.

Not only have generations of curators puzzled over the origins of the ensemble but the weapons themselves also proved difficult to identify. A closer study of the individual pieces shows that this is an exceptionally mixed collection. For many years the weapon rack was thought to have been made by or influenced by Chinese craftsmen in Batavia. This was shown, for example, by the Chinese phoenixes (*fenghuang*).[9] However, recent research suggests that the work is more Vietnamese in style.[10] The Chinese motifs used by Batavia's craftsmen are mainly those of the Chinese who came to Java from the southern provinces of China, especially Fukien. They called themselves Hokkiens. Their language differed from the Chinese lingua franca, which was Mandarin, and the decorative style of their artefacts often included Javanese and even Dutch elements. This merging of styles, which is a

---

7 Inventory of the estate of Cornelis Tromp, compiled by Notary J. van Ulenbroeck of Amsterdam, 14 April 1692. Amsterdam Maritime Museum library, J-613 (I), inv. no. 1993.0436. See also: W. Martin, 'Een en ander uit den inventaris der nalatenschap van Cornelis Tromp' *Oud-Holland* 19 (1901), 9–76.

8 For the rest, the inventory mentions only a few daggers in an iron chest with jewellery and valuables in another room. Martin (1901), 67.

9 J. van Campen and E. Hartkamp-Jonxis, *Asian Splendour: Company Art in the Rijksmuseum* (Zutphen, 2011), 59–63.

10 Information provided by Jan Veenendaal, recently published in his *Asian Art and Dutch Taste* (Zwolle/Den Haag, 2014), 93–4.

characteristic of Chinese artisans working in Batavia, is not a feature of the weapon rack, as the carvings on it are more reminiscent of the style of Indochina. This is evident on the sides of the lions' heads on the rack (figure 9). The curved forms that we see here recall the old style of carving that adorned the houses of North Vietnam in the eighteenth and nineteenth centuries.

If we accept that the rack was made in North Vietnam, in what was then Tonkin, where did the weapons originate?

As it stands today, the rack has two almost identical muskets at the top, each with its own wooden cover (figure 10).

In Wemans's list these are given as 'Two muskets, with similar mounts, in a cover'. Originally the Rijksmuseum displayed them as Turkish, and later as Japanese or Chinese, with a question mark. Japanese would have seemed more likely, given the octagonal barrels and the particular curve of the butts. Yet this style of long slender butt, curving downwards, is also characteristic of guns that were made in

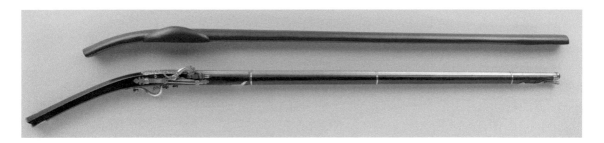

Tonkin.[11] Elsewhere in Vietnam, gunsmiths tended to make firearms in the Indo-Portuguese style. I know of no other examples of this kind of wooden cover. The Japanese made gun cases, but they contained the whole weapon and were made as a box with a lid attached by hinges: that is not the form employed here. These covers do not protect the whole gun, since they leave part of the butt unprotected. Moreover, they do not seem to have been made specifically for these muskets. They slide off and, since there are no hooks or eyes or other attachments on the wood, they were probably held in place on the weapon with a simple silk ribbon.

Below the muskets, the weapon rack displays two almost identical

Figure 10   One of the muskets from the weapon rack with its wooden cover (Rijksmuseum NG-NM-6099)

Figure 11   The bow (Rijksmuseum NG-NM-6093), quiver (6094) and wrist guards (6099-B) from the weapon rack

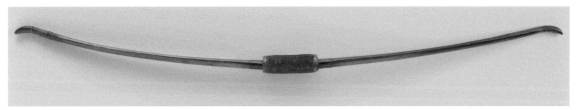

---

11 Information provided by Philip Tom, USA.

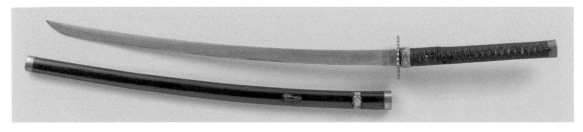

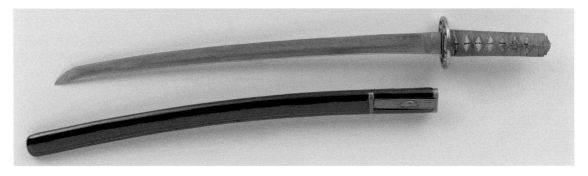

Figure 12 Swords and scabbards (Rijksmuseum NG-NM-6097-C, 6097-B and 6097-D)

bows (figure 11). Each of these features two relatively short limbs ending in nocks and meeting in a riser with a grip covered with red cloth. The nocks and risers are European in shape; the limbs are made of horn, which is a solid, though heavy, material. The limbs appear to be made in three layers, like a sandwich: one layer of horn, a central layer of wood and another layer of horn. This enabled the bowyer to exploit the strength of the horn, while not making the weapon too heavy to use. The bowstrings, which would have been made of linen or silk, have been lost.[12] Wemans also sent two quivers of arrows, each of which still contains some thirty arrows. These wooden arrows are decorated with imitations of Japanese family emblems or *mon*. The shafts are made of bamboo, and the heads are copper, while the average length is 75.5 cm.

---

12 These were already absent in the picture of the rack in the publication accompanying the exhibition of 1863.

The quiver decoration is unrelated to the ornament on the arm and wrist guards, described in the list as 'Two lead covers for the arms'.

Wrist guards are generally made of leather and should be reasonably flexible, to enable the bowman to wear them. These guards are not flexible at all and would have been practically impossible to use.

Descending further, the rack has three swords (figure 12), displayed with their scabbards. At first glance, the swords appear to be of Japanese manufacture; however, on closer inspection it can be seen that they have various features which are typically Vietnamese, or at least Southeast Asian. The two almost identical swords both have a Vietnamese style tsuba or hilt-guard and a type of tusk pommel that is often found on Vietnamese weapons. Finally, the band connecting the guard and the hilt, known as a ferrule, has Vietnamese ornament, while the way it is mounted, tapered and widening towards the guard, is also Vietnamese. When the swords were dismantled in the 1970s, some of the blades turned out to have a hole in the tang while others did not. Blades made in Southeast Asia typically do not have a hole in the tang, while Japanese blades always have a hole in the tang (figure 13). There is no hole in the tangs of any of the five pole arms.

That suggests an alternative method was used to fasten the blade to the pole or grip. The tang was embedded in a resin adhesive filling a hole bored lengthwise into the end of the shaft. The irregular surface of the tang anchored it tightly in place once the resin hardened. This was the usual way of mounting blades in Southeast Asia. The scabbards of the pole arms are made of hardwood, which suggests a Chinese influence, rather than Japanese, while the decoration of the copper mounts on the scabbards are also more reminiscent of Chinese than Japanese craftsmen (figures 14 and 15).

In conclusion then, the swords seem to have blades that are Japanese in form, yet were probably made in Vietnam or some other part of Southeast Asia. The exception is the sword with the green hilt binding, which appears to be an actual Japanese sword. The other weapons may

Figure 13   Sword blade with a tang without a hole in the Southeast Asian style (Rijksmuseum NG-NM-6097-B)

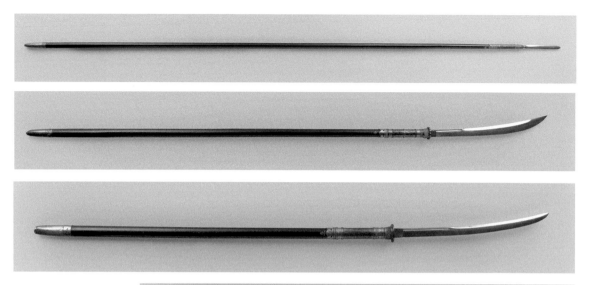

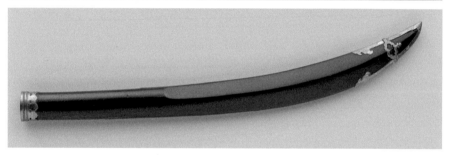

*Figure 14   Naginata
(Rijksmuseum NG-
NM-6088-A, 6089-A
and 6090-A)*

*Figure 15 Blade covers
(Rijksmuseum NG-
NM-6088-A-1, top,
6089-A-1, below)*

have been made by Japanese swordsmiths who had found themselves in Vietnam and had lost touch with their fellow craftsmen in Japan after the island went into isolation in the 1630s. Successive generations of armourers produced weapons which were basically Japanese in design, yet had all kinds of local, Vietnamese, features.

Also included in the gift were two armbands, two cartridge cases and two circular boxes for storing match (figure 16).[13]

Like the quivers, the decoration is of red lacquer with floral motifs

13 The two powder boxes, which are also mentioned in the letter, must have been lost quite early since they were never part of the ensemble at the aforementioned exhibitions.

painted in various colours, including gold. The ornamentation is similar but by no means identical. Clearly, therefore, this is not a set of matching objects. In fact, that applies to the whole ensemble. It is a thoroughly hybrid collection of objects cobbled together by Wemans to form a suite, each of the items with a different pedigree, although the whole group has a significant Vietnamese component. Moreover, the fact that the rack was not specifically made to hold weapons also underscores that the ensemble was combined from different sources.

How did a merchant in Batavia come to acquire this collection of weapons? And, more generally, what was the connection between Dutch traders and Vietnam? The Dutch had established a trading post in the kingdom of Tonkin, in today's North Vietnam, in 1637. The principal product was silk, produced locally and sold in Japan by the Dutch. The Dutch company had built up a strong position in local trade in Asia, and no Europeans were as active in this area as the Dutch in the mid-seventeenth century.[14] This was a time when the silk trade was at its height. Soon, however, it would enter a sharp decline. A second

Figure 16   Right, one of the cartridge cases (Rijksmuseum NG-NM-6092), top, one of the armbands (6099-C) and the two circuar boxes for storing match (6099-A)

---

14 The importance of this local trade in Asia can be seen from the number of VOC ships stationed permanently in Asian waters (88 out of a total of 125 in 1680); it is also evident from the Dutch company's payroll: in 1687/1688, there the VOC had 2,641 employees in Batavia alone. See J. de Jong, *De Waaier van het fortuin* (Zoetermeer, 2000), 87–8.

Dutch trading post had opened in 1637 at Faifo harbour (today's Hoi An). The main commodities here were resin lacquer and gold. Neither of these posts lasted for long. Faifo, in Quinam, closed in 1652; the Dutch continued to operate in Tonkin until 1699.[15]

Was Wemans also involved in Tonkin? What do we know about him? Unfortunately, very little. We have no record of when he went to the East Indies, what position he held or how his career developed. From his letter, it seems that Wemans had access to the corridors of power at Batavia Castle, possibly working as a merchant.

Dirk Blom, who gave him Tromp's portrait, was a member of the Council of the East Indies, the governor general's executive board in Batavia, providing administrative support, as well as checks and balances. In his letter Wemans refers to Blom as his neighbour and a good friend. Another name mentioned in the letter is that of Volckert van Goens, son of the governor general at that time, Rijcklof van Goens. Volckert was dismissed as a Batavia merchant in 1676, when he was caught trading privately. He returned to the Netherlands in November 1680.[16] These names provide a background for the circle in which Wemans lived, although they do not explain how he came into possession of the weapon rack. Apparently, when it became obvious that the portrait would not be ready on time for the fleet's return to the Netherlands at the end of the year, Wemans was forced to rustle up an alternative at short notice. Maybe the rack had been one of Van Goens's household possessions, which were doubtless auctioned off when he was forced to leave Batavia.[17] Or had Wemans acquired the rack himself at some earlier date, and decided now to give it to his friend? There is another possible hypothesis, which unfortunately lacks any substantial evidence to support it, yet which is too intriguing not to consider. A certain Johannes Besselman headed the Tonkin trading post from 1677 to 1679. In June 1679 he returned to Batavia, where he was registered as a shopkeeper from 3 March 1680. A year later he was working as a cashier at the castle.[18] Here is a direct connection linking

---

15 J. Kleinen et al., *Leeuw en draak: vier eeuwen Nederlands-Vietnamese betrekkingen* (Amsterdam, 2007).

16 National Archive, The Hague, 1.10.32 Van Goens family archive.

17 On sales of estates in Batavia, see J. Veenendaal, *Furniture from Indonesia, Sri Lanka and India during the Dutch Period* (Delft, 1985).

18 Besselman eventually died on Deshima in Japan in 1684, where he was to be the new director. Biographical details are taken from W. Wijnaendts van Resandt, *De gezaghebbers der*

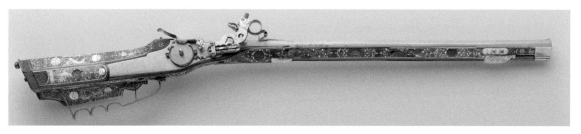

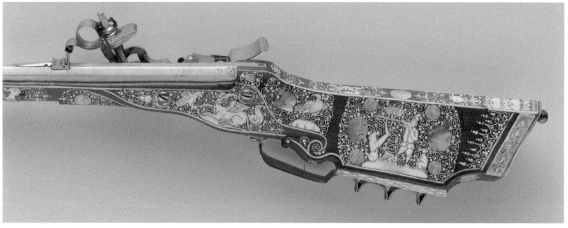

Tonkin and Batavia, precisely when Wemans was looking for a gift for Tromp. That Besselman was a man of substance is clear from his position at Tonkin and his subsequent post as cashier at the castle. The purpose of his shop in Batavia was presumably to sell products from Tonkin. Was Wemans one of his first customers in March 1680?

As we have seen, Tromp displayed the weapon rack prominently in his Amsterdam house and added weapons to the collection that he had acquired overseas, as well as his own personal weapons.[19] Among the latter were pairs of pistols by Dutch armourers Knoop, Dietemeyer and Van Eyll. The silver butt plates on the Knoop pistols are engraved with the Tromp family coat of arms. A nice example of the weapons that Tromp acquired abroad is a pair of wheellock rifles from Silesia in south Poland (figure 17). In 1656 Tromp was a rear-admiral and fighting in the Northern War against the Swedes. He

Figure 17 Pair of wheellock guns belonging to Cornelis Tromp (Rijksmuseum NG-NM-6091-B and C)

Oost-Indische Compagnie op hare buiten-comptoiren in Azie (Liebaert, 1944), 302.
19 The description of Tromp's weapons which did not appear on the rack is based largely on J. B. Kist, 'Wapens van Cornelis Tromp (1629–1691)', in *Antiek, tijdschrift voor liefhebbers van oude kunst en kunstnijverhei*d, vol. 6, no. 10: 653-673. The snaphances mentioned in the inventory were not acquired by the Rijksmuseum.

Figure 18   Portrait of Cornelis Tromp by Abraham Westervelt between 1653 and 1673 (Rijksmuseum SK–A–1683). The sword he is wearing is shown on the right (Rijksmuseum NG–NM–6095–A)

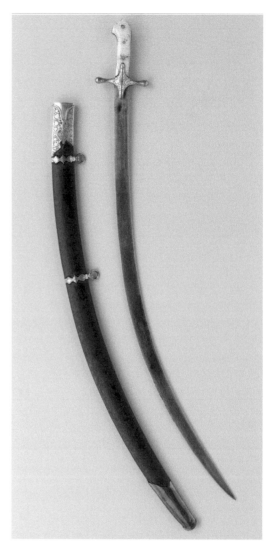

sailed around the Danzig area (modern Gdansk) off northern Poland, yet must also have found time to acquire these hunting weapons, given that they would have been hard to come by in the Netherlands in the seventeenth century. The antler, bone and mother-of-pearl decoration refers to the hunting origin, and the use for which these guns would have been intended.

The Persian sabre must have had a special significance for Cornelis Tromp. He is drawing the weapon in a portrait in which he appears as a Roman soldier, painted by artist Abraham Westervelt between 1653

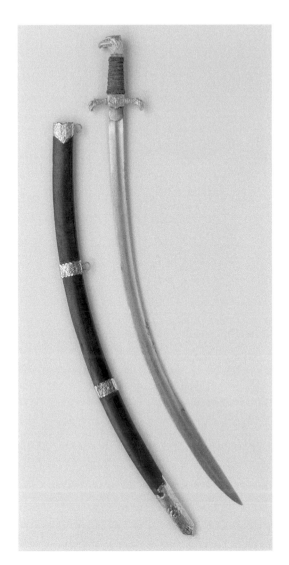

Figure 19 Portrait of Cornelis Tromp by Peter Lely, 1675 (Nederlands Scheepvaart Museum, Amsterdam). The sword he is wearing is shown on the left (Rijksmuseum NG-NM-6095-B)

and 1673 (figure 18).[20] His orange sash symbolizes his allegiance to the House of Orange and the stadholder. The sabre is a shamshir, with a walrus ivory hilt and a damascened blade. How Tromp acquired the sword is no longer known. A later portrait by Peter Lely shows Tromp with a sabre that is now also in the Rijksmuseum collection (figure 19.

It has a Persian blade, damascened, yet with a hilt that originated either in the southern Netherlands or perhaps in Italy. Together, the

---

20 See R. B. Prud'homme van Reine, 'De zeventiende-eeuwse zeeheldenportrettenreeks van Abrahma Westervelt', *Bulletin van het Rijksmuseum*, 41 (1993), 3–15.

Figure 20   Tromp's Levantine dagger, yataghan and nimcha (Rijksmuseum NG-NM-6097-A, left, 6097, centre, and 6095, right)

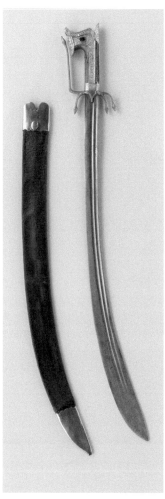

sword forms a curious combination, which must have met with Tromp's approval since he wore it in the portrait.

Finally, a few weapons from the Levant belonged to Tromp. They include a Persian dagger, a yataghan with a damascened blade and a scabbard mounted with thin silver leaf and velvet, and an Algerian nimcha with a horn and silver hilt (figure 20). Taking these weapons

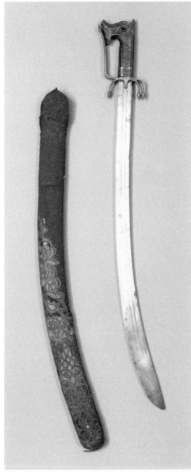

Figure 21   De Ruyter's two nimchas (Rijksmuseum NG-NM-10412, left, and 10413, right, on long-term loan to the Nederlands Scheepvaart Museum Amsterdam)

together, the link to the Dey of Algiers seems a little less fanciful. Unfortunately, however, we have no information about how Tromp came to own them.

But this is not the case with the two nimchas at the Rijksmuseum that once belonged to Michiel de Ruyter, which were acquired for the Rijksmuseum collection from his descendants. According to tradition, Michiel de Ruyter captured a nimcha from an Algerian pirate in 1655. The admiral was in the Mediterranean several times between 1644 and 1664, and his missions included punitive expeditions against Algiers, Tunis and Tripoli. The other nimcha De Ruyter apparently captured in 1657, from the French corsair captain De La Lande, who had taken it from a pirate. That would clearly make it war booty.

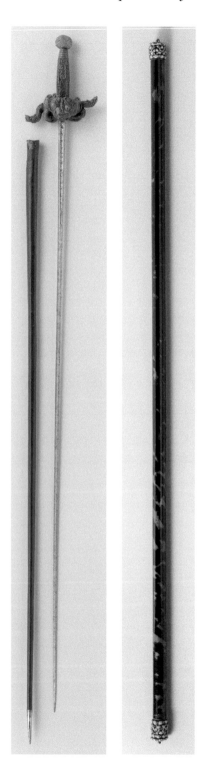

Figure 22   De Ruyter's coral-hilted rapier (Rijksmuseum NG-NM-10403) and his diamond-set baton (10402)

We also have an inventory of Michiel de Ruyter's estate which gives us an insight into the weapons he owned as well as the places he kept them.[21] De Ruyter was not especially concerned with status and style. His house was not on one of the famous Amsterdam canals, like Tromp's; he lived in a part of town where ordinary sailors lived. In the front of his house, at the entrance, which was mainly decorated with paintings, stood a rack with firearms and a model ship. The gun rack probably contained Dutch, or at least western European muskets. Like Tromp, De Ruyter also had a best room on the first floor, the main salon. In Tromp's house this was where the weapon rack was displayed. In De Ruyter's house the only weapon in the room was a presentation dagger given to De Ruyter in 1666 by the Amsterdam Admiralty. It lay in a cupboard between the napkins and the tablecloths. The only other weapons listed in the house were those kept in the fourth-floor attic in a seaman's chest: a Turkish backsword with silver mounts, which is probably one of the nimchas, and a silver dagger. It was also in this same attic that De Ruyter kept a leather pouch with a coral-hilted rapier and a baton set with diamonds (figure 22).[22]

The rapier is the only weapon in his possession which he received as a diplomatic gift. De Ruyter acquired both these pieces on his last expedition in 1675. He was older and weaker by then, but always ready to do his duty, and so off he went. His mission was to help the Spaniards subdue a rebellion fomented by the French at Messina on Sicily. Sicily and the kingdom of Naples were at that time under Spanish rule. De Ruyter and his fleet managed to beat off an attack by a French fleet in the Bay of Naples. The

---

21 P. J. Blok, 'Inventaris van De Ruyter's inboedel, opgemaakt op 22–24 maart 1677', in *Bijdragen en Mededelingen Historsch Genootschap*, vol. 49 (1928), 187–213.
22 Ibid., 'Een coraele degen en Een rotting met diamanten'.

viceroy of Naples, marquis De los Veles, expressed Spain's gratitude by giving De Ruyter several expensive presents, including this rapier with a hilt made of Neapolitan coral and a tortoiseshell staff of command, decorated with diamonds and turquoise.[23] De Ruyter was not impressed by the gifts. That previous January, he had already declined the viceroy's offer of a gold chain. More than anything else, he wanted his ships repaired and to return home. It was not to be. Another confrontation with the French followed, and he was struck by cannon shot and died a few days later.

*

The weapons which I have discussed here are all displayed in the new Rijksmuseum presentation (figure 23). Tromp's weapon rack is in the main naval gallery, as part of the seventeenth-century presentation. The other weapons are displayed in the armoury room. In the course of preparing this paper I have discussed Tromp's rack and the other weapons with many people. It has been a remarkably instructive experience and has enabled me to tell the story as we know it today. Hopefully, the remaining loose ends will also be resolved in the future.[24]

---

23 The rapier was originally meant for Don Juan d'Austria, the Spanish naval minister. See G. Brandt, *Het leven en bedrijf van den Heere Michiel de Ruyter* (Amsterdam: 4th impression, 1746), 964.
24 I would like to thank Peter Dekker (Amsterdam) and Philip Tom (USA) for sharing their knowledge and enthusiasm about the weapon rack.

The East India Company Gift to the Tower of London in 1853

Thom Richardson and Natasha Bennett

The Tower of London has been, throughout its history, a Mecca for visitors. Not all visitors came voluntarily, though. Charles, Duke of Orléans, arrived as a prisoner of war after Agincourt in 1415, providing us with the earliest illustration of the White Tower in one of his books of poetry.[1] The noted German jouster, Wilwolt von Schaumberg, is the earliest recorded diplomatic visitor, part of the embassy from Maximilian I in 1489, shown the 'many great cannon, quartans and culverins, which shoot forth balls of iron, with many other culverins and stone cannon the like of which are no longer much seen elsewhere'; soon afterwards a Venetian ambassador described 'the diligent watch that is kept now over the Tower of London was never so before the reign of Henry VII, who keeps there a great store of heavy artillery and hand guns, bombards, arquebuses and battle-axes, but not in the quantity I should have supposed'.[2] Geoffrey Parnell has shown how by the mid-1570s visitors were regularly shown round the Tower, and records the numerous descriptions of what could be seen, including the armours of Henry VIII and Charles Brandon

---

1 M. J. Arn (ed.), *Charles d'Orléans in England* (Woodbridge, 2000); British Library MS Royal 16 F. ii, f. 73.

2 'Die sie des künigs erkerei und geschütz sehen liessen, das was von mancherlai haubtgeschossen, cartanen und notschlangen, die eisen klotzen schiessen von andern schlangen vierteil und stainbüchsen, desgleichen bei einander nit vill mehr gesehen ist,' in A. von Keller (ed.), *Die Geschichten und Taten Wilwolts von Schaumberg* (Stuttgart, 1859), 96; H. Cust, *Gentlemen Errant* (London, 1909), 187–8; C. A. Sneyd (translator, from the Italian) *A Relation . . . of the Island of England . . . about the year 1500* (London, 1847), 45–6.

which would become staples of the later displays, and the artillery.[3]

The removal of the royal armours from Greenwich to the Tower in the late 1640s prepared the way for the first museum display at the Tower, the Horse Armoury (commonly but never officially referred to as the Line of Kings), which can be shown to have existed by 1652. It acquired a political edge as a demonstration of the vast historical lineage of the English monarchy with the restoration of Charles II in 1660, and was redisplayed on nice new horses in 1688–90 and moved into the first floor of the building known as New Armouries. The display was gradually expanded during the nineteenth century, when the historical inaccuracies regarding the dates of the armours and the kings they represented led to condemnation by the armour historian Samuel Rush Meyrick, and a second redisplay in the custom-built single-storey Gothic New Horse Armoury on the south side of the White Tower.[4] Meyrick's redisplay of 1825 showed how limited the collection was, and led to a new phase of acquisition to fill the major gaps, such as the profound lack of medieval European armour.[5]

The gap in the field of non-European arms and armour was even wider. By chance, only one of the two Japanese armours presented to King James I by Tokugawa Hidetada in 1613 had made its way to the Tower, and there was nothing else. The change in function at the Tower, from merely preserving the collection to expanding it, which Malcolm Mercer shows to have started as early as 1820, started the acquisition of an Asian collection as early as 1833, when the famous 'Norman Crusader', a Mughal armour of mail and plate for man and horse which started life in Tong Castle, moved to Richard Greene's museum of curiosities in Litchfield, thence to Bullock's Museum in Liverpool and then, with the addition of the horse armour, to London.[6]

---

3 G. Parnell, 'The Early History of the Tower Armouries,' *Royal Armouries Yearbook* 1 (1996), 45–52.

4 See also T. Richardson, 'The Armours in the "Line of Kings" in the Horse Armoury at the Tower,' *Arms & Armour* 10.2 (2013), 97–113.

5 See M. Mercer, 'Samuel Meyrick, the Tower Storekeepers, and the Rearrangement of the Tower's Historic Collections of Arms and Armour, c. 1821–1869,' *Arms & Armour* 10.2 (2013), 114–127.

6 T. Richardson, 'The Tong Crusader', *Country Life* (2 April 1987), 98–9, which gives the references to its long provenance history, starting with F. Grose, *A Treatise on Ancient Armour* (London, 1786), pl. 21; now xxvia.16, 23, xxvih.18; see also F. H. Cripps-Day, *A Record of Armour Sales* (London, 1925), xxxvi–vii.

Figure 1 'Firing the Tower guns on Monday night for the victories in India' (Illustrated London News, December 1846)

This took its place in the Horse Armoury, providing at last (though not for long) a medieval European mail armour. It was soon joined by an important group of medieval armour from Istanbul: following the redecoration of the Hagia Irene, just outside the Topkapı Saray, on the accession of Abdulmecid I in 1839, a great quantity of medieval Turkish (Ottoman, ak-Koyonlu and Timurid) armour was disposed of, through an Italian merchant to Genoa, and through the hands of a Genoese gentleman to Robert Curzon, Baron Zouche of Haryngworth, to the Tower by about 1840.[7] Unfortunately we have no detailed records of the acquisitions of the period. There was no museum register, and it is only with the publication of Hewitt's Catalogue of 1859 that the objects in the museum were given individual numbers. The last inventory without them, the 'Account of articles on show and ornament in and about the Horse Armoury' of 1857, lists the numbers of objects, divided

7   J. Hewitt, *Official Catalogue of the Tower Armouries* (London, 1859), 116–7; a similar account, though differing in the inclusion of Samuel Luke Pratt, the notorious armour-faker of Bord Street, in the narrative, was told by Baron de Cosson in the introduction to Sotheby's sale catalogue for the Zouche collection in 1920, Cripps-Day, *A Record of Armour Sales*, 189–90.

by location.[8] However, acquisitions of Asian arms and armour were extensive, including the Gilman gift of Chinese arms, pieces from the collections of the Duke of York and Warren Hastings, and a large purchase from the Great Exhibition of 1851.[9] By 1857 there was an Asiatic Room in the White Tower, and the collection had become a major part of the museum display.

One of the largest of these acquisitions, originally comprising nearly 200 items, was the gift of the East India Company (EIC). The impetus for the acquisition came from the Tower, and seems to have been in response to the public interest in the Sikhs following the First Anglo-Sikh War of 1845–6 (figure 1). Though the Sikh army was narrowly beaten at Mudki, failed to impose victory at Ferozshah, then lost at Aliwal, the Khalsa had impressed with its military ability. The Sikh artillery park, built up by Maharaja Ranjit Singh, was evidently a match for the artillery of the EIC, and the record of it, compiled by Captain Ralph Smyth in 1848, is evidence of that respect (figures 2 and 3).[10] The hard fought battles of the Second Anglo-Sikh War, Chillianwallah and Gujrat did nothing to reduce British respect for the Sikhs, but the treaty of Lahore also brought the entire Sikh treasury into Company hands.[11] Dr (later Sir) John Login of the Bengal Horse Artillery found himself early in 1849 Killah-ki Malik ('Lord of the Lahore Citadel'), drawing up lists of the jewels and other valuables, including 'the Diamond [Koh-i-noor]' as well as Ranjit Singh's armour, the sword of the Persian hero Rustam, and 'the armour worn by the warriors and sirdars of note, many stained with their blood'.[12]

In this one case we have evidence for active collection for the Tower. The Marquis of Anglesey as Master General of the Ordnance wrote to the Board of the EIC on 18 June 1849 requesting that

> specimens of oriental armour, particularly Afghan and Sikh, should be forwarded from India to be deposited in the National Armoury

---

8 RA Archives i.21.

9 Hewitt (1859), 102–20.

10 R. Smyth, *Plans of Ordnance Captured by the Army of Sutledge under the Command of General Sir Hugh Gough and Lieut. Gen Sir Henry Hardinge* (London, 1848); N. Carleton, 'Lions' Teeth: The Artillery of Maharaja Ranjit Singh', *Sikh Spectrum* 22 (2005), accessed at http://sikhspectrum.com/2005/11/lions-teeth-the-artillery-of-maharaja-ranjit-singh

11 L. Login, *Sir John Login and Duleep Singh* (London, 1890), 155, 159.

12 Login (1890), 182–4.

Figure 2 'The Sikh trophy guns forming up in the fort of Monghyr' (Illustrated London News, 20 March, 1847)

Figure 3 R Smyth's 'Plans of ordnance', drawings of the type of the Royal Armouries Sutlej gun XIX.329, and the accompanying catalogue of the types of Sikh artillery (Royal Armouries Library)

at the Tower of London. We are desirous that your best exertions should be used to procure as complete a set as possible of the specimens required and that they should be forwarded to us from time to time as they may be collected with full information of the countries in which they were used, their dates and other particulars of interest.[13]

The instruction was forwarded from the Court to the Governor General, by this time James, Earl of Dalhousie, and passed down the line, Colonel J. Stuart, Secretary to the Government of India, Military Dept, writing on 16 August 1849 to Major R. Wyllie with orders for Lieutenant Colonel H. J. Tucker to instruct Major General Sir Walter Raleigh Gilbert, commander of the 2nd Infantry Division at Chilianwallah, to procure the specimens.[14]

---

13 British Library, L/MIL/3/492, collection. 62, no. 1.
14 BL, L/MIL/3/492, collection. 62, no. 13.

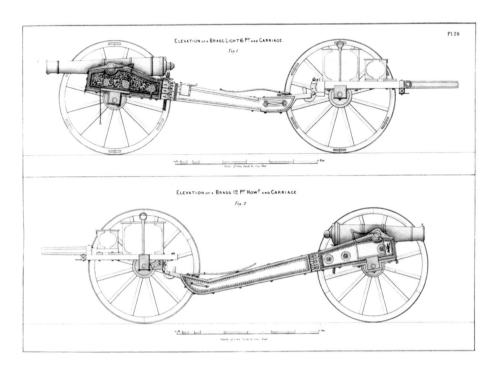

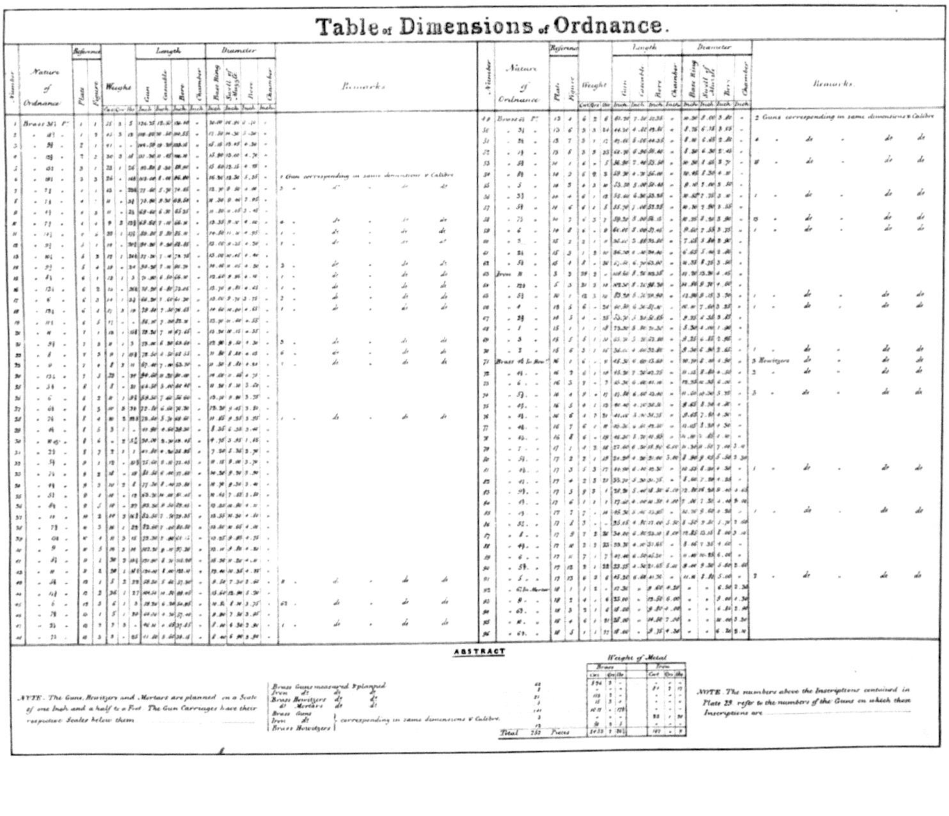

Pl 28
ELEVATION OF A BRASS LIGHT 6 P^R AND CARRIAGE
Fig. 1
Scale of One Inch to One Foot
ELEVATION OF A BRASS 12 P^R HOW^R AND CARRIAGE
Fig. 2
Scale of One Inch to One Foot

Table of Dimensions of Ordnance.

Number | Nature of Ordnance | Reference: Plate, Figure | Weight (Cwt, Qrs, lbs) | Length (Inch): Gun, Cascable, Bore, Chamber | Diameter (Inch): Base Ring, Swell of Muzzle, Bore, Chamber | Remarks

ABSTRACT

NOTE. The Guns, Howitzers and Mortars are planned on a Scale of one Inch and a half to a Foot. The Gun Carriages have their respective Scales below them.

Brass Guns measured & planned
Iron do do do
Brass Howitzers do do
do Mortars do do
Brass Guns
Iron do
Brass Howitzers
corresponding in same dimensions & Calibre.
Total 252 Pieces

Weight of Metal: Brass (Cwt, Qrs, lbs); Iron (Cwt, Qrs, lbs)

NOTE. The numbers above the Inscriptions contained in Plate 29 refer to the numbers of the Guns on which these Inscriptions are

Dr Login, meanwhile, as well as cataloguing the jewels, had compiled an extensive list of the arms and armour. As Ian Bottomley has pointed out, the details are too brief easily to identify individual items.[15] However, they include the arms of all the principal Sikh leaders, the late Ranjit Singh, whose possessions included the sword he usually wore, with its Persian blade mounted and jewelled in Lahore with an agate hilted by-knife and 205 diamonds, valued at Rs 13,700, a silver bungalow valued at Rs 35,000 and the state chair at Rs 16,000, as well as an armour comprising three pieces, *pyjama*, *koortee* and *topee* (mail chausses, shirt and helmet), valued at Rs 200 and made in Lahore, with a plume or *khalgi* valued at Rs 368, some more swords, bow, quiver, powder horn and belt, two matchlocks, two shields, a small drum and a swordstick (*gupti*).[16] Maharaja Kharak Singh (1801–40) contributed a similar armour, but made in Delhi, three swords, a shield and four matchlocks, and there is a long list of pieces formerly belonging to Maharaja Sher Singh (1807–42); Dhian Singh; Raja Hira Singh; the fakir Nur ud-Din, member of Dalip Singh's regency council; Hari Singh Nalwa, former leader of the Khalsa; Sardar Jowala Singh, supporter of Sher Singh killed in 1841, whose former possessions included the *khalgi* of the last Guru, Govind;[17] and pieces taken by the Sikhs in the recent past such as the sword worth Rs 10,000 of the Mahratta leader Jaswant Rao Holkar; the sword of Fathi Khan, Wazir of Kabul, killed in 1818; and a sword valued at Rs 17,000 belonging to Nau Nihal Singh, the 'sword of the Persian hero Rustam taken from Shah Shuja, with a Persian blade mounted and jewelled' with 57 emeralds, 437 diamonds and 70 garnets in Lahore recorded by Login in his inventory of the Toshakhana and letters home.[18] The list is transcribed as an appendix to this paper.

---

15 I. Bottomley, 'A tentative classification of Indian firearms,' *Royal Armouries Yearbook 7* (2002), 77–83.

16 For details of the sword, see Login's detailed account of the Toshakana, BL, L/PS/5/202, no. 61. The state chair, made by the goldsmith Hafeez Muhammad Multani, is now V&A 2518(IS).

17 Sue Strong records that Dalhousie preserved this important group of Sikh objects together; they were preserved at Colstoun House, and returned to the government of India in 1965, 'The Sikh treasury', in K. Brown, *Sikh Art and Literature* (Abingdon, 1999), 61.

18 Copied in a letter from Major G. H. MacGregor, Deputy Commissioner of Lahore, to Major A. P. Burn, Deputy Secretary to the Board of Administration, 20 February 1850, BL, L/MIL/3/492, collection 62, no. 38, ff. 30–34; BL, L/PS/5/202, no. 61; Lord Egerton of Tatton suggested that 3391(IS) was the 'sword of Rustam' in his *Indian Arms and Armour* (London, 1896), 131, no. 646.

Major General Gilbert was, however, not such a rapid correspondent. When pressed he eventually replied to Colonel Tucker:

> I beg you will inform his excellency the Commander in Chief that I personally had no means of collecting, as public funds from which to pay for the specimens of arms and armour required were lacking.[19]

In the event, Dalhousie himself undertook to make the selection when he visited Lahore on 28 November 1851; Login was ordered by Herbert Edwardes to water the roads in advance of His Excellency's visit, but Dalhousie was positively congratulatory in his praise of Login's work in Lahore.[20]

We have no detailed information about the arrival of the EIC gift at the Tower, and the list that accompanied the gift does not survive, but by 1857 it was on display in the new Asiatic Room in the White Tower, in a large case inscribed in gold letters 'Armour, arms and equipment of the northern frontier of India presented by the Hon East India Co., anno domini 1853'.

Despite the lack of documentation regarding the arrival of the EIC gift at the Tower, we do have a near contemporary source from 1859 which seems likely to be the closest approximation to any original inventory of the contents. John Hewitt's *Official Catalogue of the Tower Armouries* introduced Class XV, 'Asiatic Arms and Armour, Horse-Furniture, &c.; including the weapons of the Turks and of the Arabs of the North Coast of Africa', with the following explanation:

> A large portion of the Indian armour and weapons was presented to the national collection by the Hon. East India Company. This princely donation was accompanied by a series of documents, compiled in the various presidencies of India, authenticating the objects contributed, and stating with minute exactness the places where they were made and the races by whom they had been used. The value of this information, relating to a country so distant, and to a class of objects so little the subject of study at home, will be readily appreciated by all who have given to such topics the smallest amount of consideration. It has therefore been thought desirable,

---

19 BL, L/MIL/3/492, collection 62, no. 42.
20 Ibid., no. 5; Login (1890), 187. Dalhousie's list is transcribed as Appendix 2 below.

in the description of Asiatic productions here offered, to keep apart the portion forming the donation of the East India Company.[21]

Hewitt then presented an itemized list of the gift objects, setting them out according to area of origin and the peoples with whom they were associated, which suggests he was copying the information from the documents that he mentioned in his introduction. Unfortunately the series of documents which accompanied the gift cannot now be found, but it does highlight the importance of the gift: not only does it record the areas from which the pieces came, but also their local names, and Hewitt's terminology for Indian arms and armour has been essentially followed in subsequent publications.

The groupings run as follows: Arms of the Mahrattas (subdivided into sections for cavalry and infantry); Sikh arms in use by the Sardars (chiefs) in the Punjab; Afghan [*sic*] arms and accoutrements; arms and armour from Rajpootana, from Oedeypore [Udaipur], from Jodhpore, from Indore, from Hyderabad, from Bootea (S.W. frontier of Bengal); arms of the Akalees; arms of the Kookis of North Cachar, Presidency of Bengal; arms of the Mishmee Garrows; Angami-Naga arms; arms from Keddah – presented by the Rajah of Keddah; from Malacca and the Eastern Archipelago, Malay; from Palembang; from Bencoolen; from Borneo; from Java.[22] There is a broad correlation between the ordering of the categories and the quantity of material gathered for each group. The Mahrattas, the Sikhs, the Afghans and the Rajputs are placed as the first entries, and are populated by greater numbers of objects; the representation is reduced as the catalogue moves on to consider the smaller, dispersed tribes or more localised areas of governance, such as the Nagas or the inhabitants of the Straits settlements. This seems to be a logical reflection of proportionate influence, at least from the point of view of the Tower and the EIC. This presentation of a greater concentration of arms and armour from the larger, more powerful native empires whose territories had been brought under British supervision reinforces the theory already expounded in the first part of this paper, that the impetus behind this gift was triggered by a growing interest and awareness among home

---

21 Hewitt (1859), 92.
22 Ibid., 93–102.

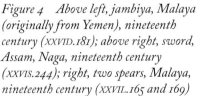

Figure 4   Above left, jambiya, Malaya (originally from Yemen), nineteenth century (XXVID.181); above right, sword, Assam, Naga, nineteenth century (XXVIS.244); right, two spears, Malaya, nineteenth century (XXVIL.165 and 169)

audiences about Indian populations who had provided significant, publicized resistance to British rule.

Unfortunately, many of the original gift objects are no longer in the collections of the Royal Armouries due to the vicissitudes of the Oriental collection under different authorities at the Tower and the temporary wholesale removal of non-European items to the British Museum from 1914 until after the Second World War. This is especially true of the armour and weaponry that was sourced from South East Asia and the lesser known Indian tribes; out of a tally of around fifty-two assorted staff weapons, knives and daggers, swords, shields and archery equipment that were presented from these areas, we can now only identify one Naga sword and a jambiya and three spears from Malaysia (figure 4). Happily, we do still have a reasonable selection of objects drawn the most prominent sections in Hewitt's catalogue; the Mahrattas, the Sikhs (including the Akalees), the Afghans, Rajasthan and the Deccan, which give a good indication of the character of the gift as a whole. The East India Company correspondence already discussed relates to the process of sourcing the Sikh and Afghan components of the gift, and provides interesting evidence of the methods by which the material was chosen and collected. This helps us to see these objects as an integrated group, rather than a melange of rich artefacts thrown together with little to connect them.

Hewitt's catalogue of the gift objects begins with the Mahrattas, accompanied by the explanatory note 'The arms are such as would be worn by Chiefs and the higher classes of soldiery in the Mahratta service'.[23] The section starts with a range of weaponry associated with cavalry, including a sword, daggers, a spear, a composite bow, a quiver and arrows, a matchlock musket, a shield, and armour. This is followed by a similar selection for infantry, including a sword, a spear, a musket, daggers, archery equipment, a *bagh nakh* or tiger's claw, a shield and a mail shirt and hood. The majority of these Mahratta items were from Gwalior; a matchlock musket, a spear, two daggers and the *bagh nakh* were recorded as having been made at Lashkar in Gwalior, the arm defences have a Nagari inscription recording that they were made at Shahjahanabad, or Old Delhi, and another matchlock and some of the mail was manufactured at Narwar in Madhya Pradesh (figures 5–7).[24] It is interesting that Hewitt had faith that the provenances he was recording were sufficiently accurate to declare. This is also the only source area for the gift that is divided into separate sections for cavalry and infantry, which implies he must have had some reason to differentiate here. We no longer have the original documentation for the Mahratta grouping, or all of the objects, so it is difficult to state with certainty that Hewitt's assertions were accurate. As we have seen above, the Master General of the Ordnance was keen to collect material systematically and with full details. If the same methods of collection were employed for the rest of the gift, then Hewitt was probably copying out his provenance information verbatim.

---

23 Hewitt (1859), 93.
24 Professor H. H. Wilson of the India Office, who read the inscriptions for Hewitt, misread the date on the matchlock XXVIF.126/xv.6 as 1786 and interpreted it as Vikrama rather than Śaka era, leading him to date it improbably to 1649 rather than 1784.

The next section is entitled 'Sikh arms, in use by the Sirdars (chiefs) in the Punjab'.[25] This covers a similar span of armour and weaponry, although regional flavour emerges in form and decoration. There was a sword, a spear, a shield, a composite bow, various quivers and arrows, a matchlock musket, a *kamar*, mail shirts, *chahar a'ineh* (a four-plate cuirass), arm defences, helmets and horse equipment (figure 8). Hewitt's

25 Hewitt (1859), 95.

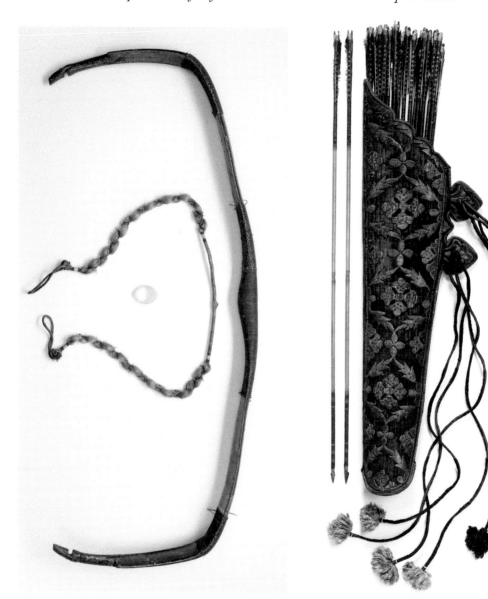

Figure 6   Composite bow, thumb ring and bowstring, Gwalior, nineteenth century (XXVIB.8, 103) and quiver and arrows, Gwalior, eighteenth century (XXVIB.32)

choice of subtitle for the group shows that some of these pieces may well match items from Dr Login's group of armour and arms recorded as having belonged to and been worn by the 'late Maharajas and Sirdars etc of the Punjab',[26] or the Governor General's subsequent selection from the Toshakhana in Lahore.[27] Both of these lists recorded the individual

26 BL, L/MIL/3/492, collection. 62, no. 50.
27 BL, IOR P/199/22, no. 111.

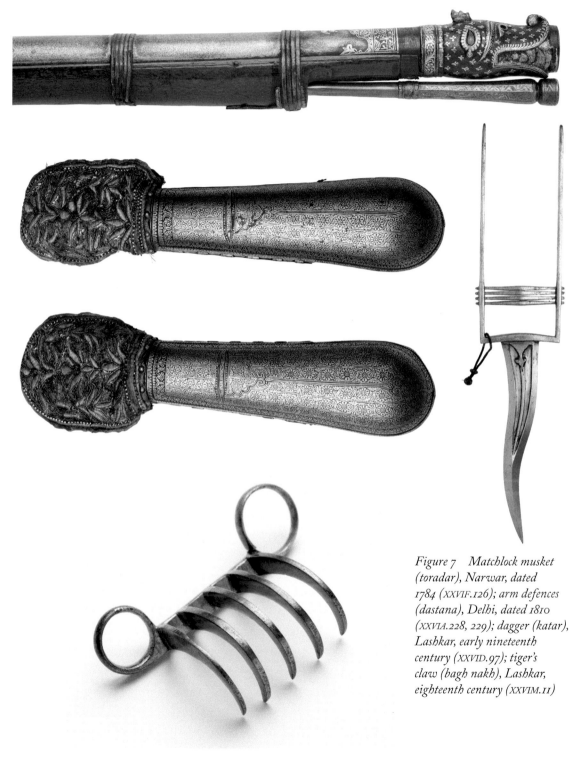

Figure 7   Matchlock musket (toradar), Narwar, dated 1784 (XXVIF.126); arm defences (dastana), Delhi, dated 1810 (XXVIA.228, 229); dagger (katar), Lashkar, early nineteenth century (XXVID.97); tiger's claw (bagh nakh), Lashkar, eighteenth century (XXVIM.11)

Figure 8 Sword (talwar), scabbard and belt, Lahore, nineteenth century (XXVIS.138); matchlock musket (toradar), possibly of Ranjit Singh, Lahore, early nineteenth century (XXVIF.42)

Sikhs who had previously owned the armour and weapons. The sets usually included armour, a sword and a shield from each named person, although some incorporated more items such as matchlocks or archery equipment. Unfortunately, the descriptive details that came through to Hewitt were apparently sparse and generic. No finalized list exists of what was ultimately received from the EIC, and many of the gift items ended up either in the Royal Collection or at the Museum of the East India Company which was absorbed by the Victoria and Albert Museum in 1879. Out of those objects which did come to the Tower Armouries many were never recovered from the British Museum. However, there are certain items still remaining within collection of the Royal Armouries for which an appropriate description occurs only once in the Sikh sections of the Hewitt catalogue, and once in the

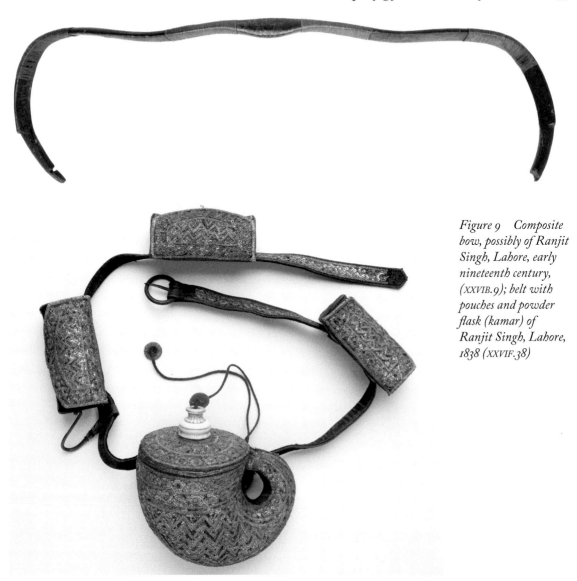

Figure 9   Composite bow, possibly of Ranjit Singh, Lahore, early nineteenth century, (XXVIB.9); belt with pouches and powder flask (kamar) of Ranjit Singh, Lahore, 1838 (XXVIF.38)

EIC draft lists of Sikh arms and armour (see appendices). Therefore, a tentative provenance can be drawn from these objects back to named individuals, which has the potential to be an exciting, albeit uncertain, new lead. For example, by a process of elimination the composite bow and *kamar* were probably associated with Maharaja Ranjit Singh, and were made in the Toshakhana of Lahore to order, in the case of the *kamar* for the wedding of Kharak Singh in 1838 (figure 9).[28] The *chahar*

28   BL, IOR P/199/22, no. III; S. Stronge, *The Arts of the Sikh Kingdoms* (London, 1999), 89.

*Figure 10
Cuirass (chahar
a'ineh) and helmet
(top), possibly
of Sher Singh,
Lahore, early
nineteenth century
(XXVIA.5); left,
spear with hunting
scenes, possibly
of Jowala Singh,
Lahore, early
nineteenth century
(XXVIL.221)*

a'ineh and helmet is likely to be the armour recorded by both Login and Dalhousie as the property of Maharaja Sher Singh, and the spear with painted hunting scenes seems to have belonged to Sardar Jowala Singh (figure 10). There is obviously a risk involved in attributing these illustrious yet spurious provenances to specific items. We have already seen that Hewitt recorded provenance diligently where he could, so it is unlikely that he would have missed an opportunity to include direct associations had they been provided. On the other hand we have no

Figure 11   Left, quoit turban (dastar bungga),
Lahore, eighteenth century (XXVIA.60); right, powder
flask and pouches (kamar), Lahore, early nineteenth
century (XXVIF.97)

idea how much information from the notes of Login or Dalhousie was
presented in the final, lost records of what the Tower received. Also,
the fact that Hewitt chose to separate these arms of the Sikh sardars
from a later section devoted to the Akali Sikhs provides another
indication that they were the same personal arms that Login listed in
his inventory. According to Hewitt's catalogue, the second Sikh group
originally contained some similar weapons to the sardars' section, such
as swords, daggers, a matchlock musket and a *kamar* along with objects
predominantly identified with the Akalis such as the famous *dastar
bungga*, or quoit turban (figure 11).[29] Yet both groups were synonymous
with the Sikh armed forces, so it seems that Hewitt intentionally
emphasized the distinction between the specialist equipment of the
Nihangs and the richer accoutrements of individual Sikh chiefs.

---

29 Hewitt (1859), 98–9.

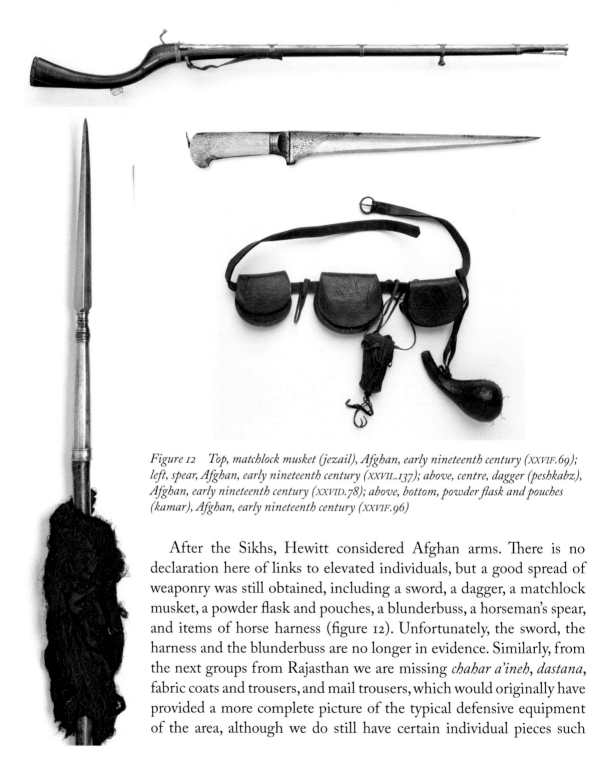

Figure 12   Top, matchlock musket (jezail), Afghan, early nineteenth century (XXVIF.69); left, spear, Afghan, early nineteenth century (XXVIL.137); above, centre, dagger (peshkabz), Afghan, early nineteenth century (XXVID.78); above, bottom, powder flask and pouches (kamar), Afghan, early nineteenth century (XXVIF.96)

After the Sikhs, Hewitt considered Afghan arms. There is no declaration here of links to elevated individuals, but a good spread of weaponry was still obtained, including a sword, a dagger, a matchlock musket, a powder flask and pouches, a blunderbuss, a horseman's spear, and items of horse harness (figure 12). Unfortunately, the sword, the harness and the blunderbuss are no longer in evidence. Similarly, from the next groups from Rajasthan we are missing *chahar a'ineh*, *dastana*, fabric coats and trousers, and mail trousers, which would originally have provided a more complete picture of the typical defensive equipment of the area, although we do still have certain individual pieces such as this helmet with the nasal guard and impressive plumes (figure 13).[30]

As Hewitt's geographical focus moved south from Indore to Hyderabad, many catalogue entries shifted from recording individual pieces of armour or weaponry, which together made up an overview of the equipment used in different areas, to assimilating entire related sets within one description (although individual museum numbers are maintained and set down as a range). Hewitt lists two main sets from both Indore and Hyderabad, along with some separate entries for spears and a long bow from Indore. We still have some of the pieces from one of the Indore compilations; originally it consisted of a coat of mail, a cuirass made from strips of hinged steel, a pair of arm defences, a round shield of buffalo hide, a *khanda* with peacocks on the blade and a dagger with an embossed blade; the objects shown here represent the elements we can still identify (figure 14). Similarly, we still have the *chahar a'ineh* and helmet from one Hyderabad group, although not the accompanying coat of mail, arm defences, shield and mace. Happily, the other Hyderabad set has remained complete, and probably gives the best impression of the comprehensive span of regional material that the gift contents covered. It is still displayed as a group, and includes a cuirass with breast and backplate of the type that was common in the Deccan, a pair of *dastana*, a helmet with a Quranic inscription on the nasal guard, a shield of embossed steel and a steel mace (figure 15).[31] Again, although we have no documentation which specifically details the process of collection from this area of India, the assembly of groups of objects such as this continued to reflect the determination

Figure 13   Helmet (top), Rajasthan, 18th century (XXVIA.58)

30 Hewitt (1859), 98–9.
31 Ibid.

Figure 14 Sword (khanda), Indore, late eighteenth century (XXVIS.34); dagger (chilanum), Indore, early nineteenth century (XXVID.73) cuirass, Indore, seventeenth century (XXVIA.21)

expressed elsewhere in the East India Company correspondence for 'as complete a set as possible' of Indian arms and armour.

*

The gift of the East India Company helped the developing national armoury at the Tower to illustrate the arms and armour of a recent series of conflicts on the far side of the world to a public agog for news from India, but also reinforced the idea that the Company was the legitimate government of the country with the authority to abstract such collections and send them home for the education of the public. Within five years of the gift the de facto rule of the EIC had become reality: the suppression of the Sepoy Mutiny had called into question the ability of the Company to administrate such a vital imperial possession, and allowed Disraeli to have Queen Victoria crowned

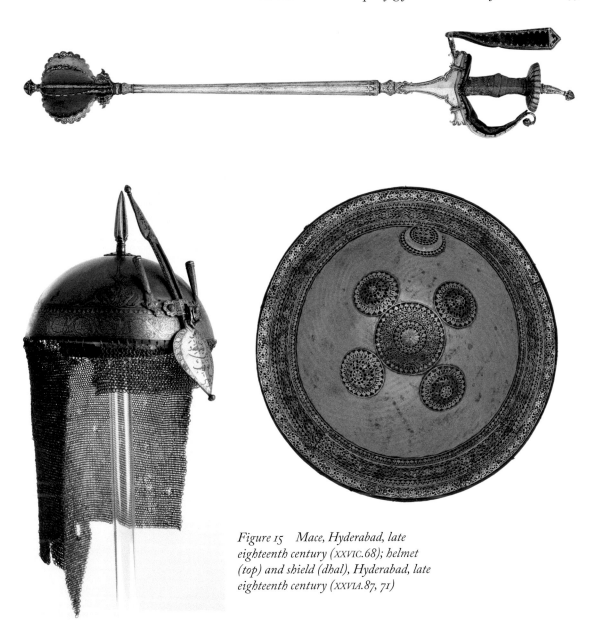

Figure 15   Mace, Hyderabad, late eighteenth century (XXVIC.68); helmet (top) and shield (dhal), Hyderabad, late eighteenth century (XXVIA.87, 71)

as Empress of India. By the standards of the time the EIC gift to the Tower was effectively a diplomatic gift from one government to another, like so many of the gifts discussed at this conference.

Appendix 1: Dr Login's list[32]

I have the honour to forward herewith for the information of the Board a copy of the list submitted to the Most Noble the Governor General of India by Dr Login or armour and arms selected as having been worn by the late Maharajas and sirdars etc of the Punjab.

Maharajah Ranjit Singh

A suit of armour consisting of 3 pieces, pyjama, koortee and topee: Rs. 200, made in Lahore, valued by Uzeemullah armourer

Keilge or plume for helmet: Rs 368

Swords, jewelled, 2 (nos 82 and 14): Rs 150

A bow and quiver of arrows, 2: Rs 448

Powder horn with belt and pouches: Rs 252[33]

Matchlocks, 2 (nos 22, Rs 1,720 and no. 64, Rs 180): Rs. 1,900

Shields, jewelled, 2: Rs 2,500

A small drum and tabarzeen: Rs 1,000, valued by Banyaun goldsmith, made by his father.

Swordstick (gooptee): Rs 15

Maharajah Kurrick Singh

A suit of armour of 3 pieces, pyjama, koortee and topee, with plume for helmet, 4: Rs. 130, made in Delhi, valued by Uzeemullah

Swords, 3 (no 131, Rs. 84, no. 135, Rs. 30 and no. 83, Rs. 420): Rs. 534

Shield: Rs. 50

Guns/matchlocks, 4 (no. 1, Rs. 470, no. 62, Rs. 500, no. 5, Rs. 470, no. 15, Rs. 100): Rs. 2,400

Maharajah Sher Singh

A suit of armour complete, consisting of four body plates, a pair of grieves [*sic*], helmet and shield, a coat of mail and pyjamas to match, 10: Rs. 150

Swords, 3 (no. 116, Rs. 492, no. 672, Rs. 365, no. 139, Rs. 104): Rs. 961

Shields, 2: Rs. 100

Matchlocks, 2 (no. 74, Rs. 110, no. 34, Rs. 85): Rs. 195

Kour Hownchal Singh

A suit of 3 pieces, koortee, pyjama, topee, 3: Rs. 100

Swords, 2 (no. 124, Rs. 25 and no. 74, Rs. 19): Rs. 44

Shield: Rs. 500

---

32 This is the version transcribed in the Fort William Military Dept correspondence, BL, L/MIL/3/492, collection, 62, no. 38, ff. 30–34, spellings as there.

33 See Stronge, *The Arts of the Sikh Kingdoms*, 87–9; another version of Dr Login's list including his comments shows that this *kamar* was made to order in the Toshakhana in 1838 for the marriage of his son Kharak Singh.

Raja Dhian Singh
   A suit of armour of 3 pieces, koortee, pyjama and topee, 3: Rs. 100, made in Delhi
   Swords, 2 (no. 4, Rs. 500, no. 75, Rs. 20): Rs. 520
   Shield: Rs. 100

Raja Hira Singh
   A suit of armour of 3 pieces, koortee, pyjama and topee, 3: Rs. 80
   Sword, no.116: Rs. 40, made in Nauzanghur
   Shield: Rs. 50

Nuar ooddeen Singh, son of Maharaja Holab Singh
   Sword no. 122: Rs. 36
   Shield: Rs. 15

Sirdar Hurree Singh Nalua
   A suit of armour of 3 pieces, koortee, pyjama and topee, 3: Rs. 80
   Swords, 2 (no. 46, Rs. 190, no. 142, Rs. 50): Rs. 240
   Shield: Rs 250

Sirdar Selub Singh Sinderwallia
   A suit of armour of 3 pieces, koortee, pyjama and topee, 3: Rs. 40
   Swords, 2 (no. 117, Rs. 40, no. 118, Rs. 40): Rs. 80
   Shield: Rs. 50

Sirdar Ujul Singh Sinderwallia
   A suit of armour of 3 pieces, koortee, pyjama and topee, 3: Rs. 40
   Swords, 2 (no. 119, Rs. 40, no. 120, Rs. 94): Rs. 134
   Shield: Rs. 50

Sirdar Jorwall Singh Bahronia Gooroo Govind
   Sword no. 12: Rs. 420
   Goorroo standard or flag: Rs. 4
These arms etc. in great veneration by the Maharaja, Rajput, a Brahmin, was employed
to worship the sword at a certain hour daily receiving a jhagee for the duty, for the
kulgee or plume the Maharaja gave a village in Jahur of the yearly value of Rs. 500
   Spear: Rs. 5
   Sword: Rs. 95
   Shield: Rs. 10
   Dha or hatchet: Rs. 5
   Plume kulgee: Rs. 2
   Quoit chucker: Rs. 1

Raja Suohet Singh
   A suit of armour of 3 pieces, koortee, pyjama and topee, 3: Rs. 150
   Swords, 2 (no. 18, Rs. 1,128, no. 149, Rs. 900): Rs. 2,012
   Shield: Rs. 50

Jaswent Roy Hulkur
Sword no. 3: Rs. 10,000

Wuzuur Futteh Khan
Sword no. 3: Rs. 7,500

Surfura Khan
Sword no. 9: Rs. 3,100

Roostum
Sword no. 1: Rs. 200

Maharaja Ranjit Singh
Sword no. 2: Rs. 13,700[34]

Nour Nowree Hal Singh
Sword no. 1: Rs. 17,000[35]

Sirdar Hurree Singh Nalwa
Sword no. 4: Rs. 9,000

Dewan Kirparan
Sword no. 13: Rs. 700

Guroo Govind Singh
Sword no. 95: Rs. 18

Maharaja Ranjit Singh
Swords, 2 (no. 48: Rs. 200, no. 60, Rs. 500): Rs. 700
Silver bungalow: Rs. 35,000
State chair: Rs. 16,000

I am given to understand that in the column of remarks of the list sent to Govt. almost every item was commented on by Dr Login in the manner shown opposite Guroo Govind, but no correct record of these remarks being forthcoming I am obliged to submit the column blank.

G. M. MacGregor
Lahore citadel, 28 Feb 1851

---

34 Sword 'mounted and jewelled in Lahore and a dagger with an agate handle attached and frequently worn by Maharaja Ranjit Singh', with 205 diamonds; BL, L/PS/5/202, no. 61.
35 'Sword, Persian blade, supposed to have belonged to Shah Sooja, was taken by Maharaja Ranjit Singh and mounted and jewelled in Lahore with Hindustanee guard and handle', with 57 emeralds, 437 diamonds and 70 garnets; BL, L/PS/5/202, no. 61.

Appendix 2: Lord Dalhousie's selection[36]

List of arms and armour selection by the most noble the governor general of India from the late Lahore Durbar Toshikhana for Her Majesty Queen Victoria.

Fort William, 27 December 1850

List no. 1

1. Maharaja Shere Sing, pyjama, kortee & topee
2. Ditto, back & breast pieces, arms pieces. Manufactured in Nurwargar, polished and repaired in Lahore. These are said to have belonged originally to Shah Shoojoul Mulk & were procured from his confiscated property by Maharaja Ranjit Sing.
3. Ditto, shield inlaid in gold. Maid (sic) in Delhi and purchased from a merchant in the same place.
4. Maharaja Ranjeet Sing, sword. Presented by Jaswant Ray Holkar on his flight into the Lahore territory after having been overthrown and pursued by British forces under Lord Lake.
5. Ditto, bow. Purchased from Kurreewalla, Lahore.
6. Ditto, quiver of arrows. Made to order in the Toshikhana.
7. Ditto, powder horn. It was made in the Toshikhana on the occasion of Maharaja Kurruck Sing's marriage.
8. Ditto, matchlock, double barrelled. Bought by Deccan Moteeram from Mooltan.
9. Ditto, drum. Made by Hafiz zurger (goldsmith) Mooltanee in the Toshikhana. It is carried at the saddle for inducing battle.

List no. 2

10. Maharaja Kurruck Sing, pyjama, kortee & topee. Manufactured at Delhi and purchased from a Cashmere merchant Mendhujo.
11. Ditto, kulgee. Made to order in the Toshikhana.
12. Ditto, sword, Luckee. So-called in consequence of it having been preferred to a lac of Rs. by one of two brothers on the division of their patrimony & it was from the confiscated property of Josh Sing Ramgurda.
13. Ditto, matchlock. Brought by Deccan Moteeram from Mooltan.
14. Maharaja Ranjeet Sing, shield. Purchased from Golab Sing Mubersuria & mounted to order in the Toshikhana

---

36 BL, IOR P/199/22, no. 111. There are three separate lists in this document, these two and a list of items presented to the Prince of Wales by Maharaja Dulip Singh. The request for groups of arms and armour for the Tower Armoury and for the East India Company Museum are found in parallel throughout the correspondence relating to the selection of material from Lahore; as the Tower was one of the royal palaces in 1850 and a gift to it could quite well be seen as a gift to the queen, and because the list of items matches very closely what was acquired by the Tower, it seems most likely that the first was the Tower gift list.

List of arms and armour selection by the most noble the governor general of India from the late Lahore Durbar Toshikhana for the honourable the Court of Directors.

Set no. 1
1. Rajah Soochet Sing, pyjama, koortee & topee. Manufactured at Lahore.[37]
2. Ditto, sword (no. 148). Purchased from Cabul merchant and mounted to order.[38]
3. Ditto, shield. Purchased from Lahore merchant at Amritsar on the occasion of the Dussara.
4. Ditto, matchlock.

Set no. 2
1. Maharaja Nowarhal Sing, pyjama, koortee & topee. Manufactured at Lahore.
2. Ditto, sword (no. 124). Purchased and mounted in the Toshikhana to order.
3. Ditto Duleep Sing, shield. Made to order in the Toshikhana.
4. Ditto, matchlock (no. 74). Manufactured in Lahore and ornamented in the Toshikhana.

---

37 The mail shirt (*koortee*), helmet (*topee*) and shield are presumably V&A 3441(IS), 3421–4(IS) and 3440(IS), two of which are still associated with Suchet Singh and all of which were transferred from the India Museum in 1879.
38 Presumably V&A 3444(IS).

The Gift of the Dardanelles Gun by Abdulaziz to Queen Victoria

Nicholas Hall

The Great Turkish Bombard, also known as the 'Dardanelles Gun', in the Royal Armouries collection is one of the most impressive and fascinating pieces of artillery to survive from the Middle Ages. It was cast in 1464 for Sultan Mehmet II, the conqueror of Constantinople. According to the beautiful calligraphic muzzle inscription, which

Figure 1 The Great Turkish Bombard or Dardanelles gun in situ at the Tower of London (XIX.164)

Figure 2   The Great Turkish Bombard, details showing the screw, the calligraphic muzzle inscription and the cannon balls

commences with an appeal to Allah, it was cast by Munir Ali in the month of Rajab 868 for Mehmet Khan, son of Murad. An inscription on the chamber gives instructions for loading, referring to a powder charge of about 22.5 kg. Cast in two parts, which screw together, its length complete is about 5.2 m, weighing about 16 tonnes.[1] The calibre is about 635 mm, for stone projectiles of about 306 kg. The reduced bore of the separate powder chamber is only 230 mm. The reasons for casting it in two parts is not discussed in detail in this paper, nor its possible ballistic performance.[2] Despite the difficulty in producing the threads, casting in two parts would certainly have made the manufacture of the bombard easier. If it was unscrewed for loading, which I believe it was, the loading drill probably would have been more convenient.

The bombard was on display at the Royal Artillery Museum Woolwich from its arrival until 1929. During the 1920s there was major reorganization of military collections in London. As a result of this some important objects were transferred from Woolwich to the Tower. In 1989, during the development of the Royal Armouries museum of artillery at Fort Nelson, the bombard was moved there from the Tower, where it is been displayed under cover, having previously lived outdoors for all its life.

It would be easy to suggest that the acquisition of the great bombard was simply an aspect of British imperial greed for the treasures of the exotic Orient – an appetite a weaker power, such as Turkey, could be compelled to satisfy. More generously we might see this acquisition as an example of the well-known Victorian impulse for codification and classification, the gathering of vast collections of objects comparable to the garnering of specimens for scientific, taxonomic, purposes for the Natural History Museum. But the story of how the bombard came to England is a little more complicated. The two figures who seem to me central to this story were General Sir Henry Lefroy, KCMG, CB, FRS (1817–90) and Sultan Abdulaziz of Turkey (1830, r. 1861–76).

Few now will have heard of Lefroy. On his own he hardly could have persuaded the Turkish government to part with this imposing relic of Mehmet the Conqueror. But Lefroy's persistence was crucial,

---

1   H. L. Blackmore, *The Armouries of the Tower of London: 1, The Ordnance* (London, 1976), catalogue no 242.
2   N. Hall, 'Tudor naval gunnery: Range trials using replica ordnance', in *ICOMAM Conference October 2009 Proceedings* (Leeds, 2012), 59–64.

Figure 3 'Scene in the Northwest', a portrait of Captain John Henry Lefroy by Paul Kane, about 1845, Glenbow Museum

and something of his persona can be derived from Paul Kane's romantic painting of him (figure 3).

John Henry Lefroy was born in Hampshire in 1817. He entered the Royal Military Academy at Woolwich in 1831, where both Royal Artillery and Royal Engineer cadets were trained. If somewhat out of date in military doctrine, the curriculum was broad; it was then the only professional education provided for the British army. He was commissioned in 1834 and retired with the rank of general. Lefroy's intelligence and application resulted in his becoming a noted scientist. He became involved in the world-wide study of terrestrial magnetism; his observations produced very valuable results. Much of this work took place in Canada. When he left, the Toronto elite described Lefroy as 'a man of singularly attractive personality; a fellow of the Royal Society, he was at the same time a man of simple piety . . . his gentlemanly bearing and affable manners endeared him to us all.'[3] He was sent to Constantinople in 1855 to help with military hospital arrangements at Scutari. In contrast to the British

---

3 A. Thompson, 'Sir Henry Lefroy 1817–1890', an article written for the Canadian Meteorological and Oceanographic Society, accessed at http://www.cmos.ca/Metphotos/MSCHeads/LeFroy.pdf, 4.

ambassador, far from falling out with Florence Nightingale, she and Lefroy became friends. Lefroy visited the Dardanelles in December 1855 and saw the ancient guns there. The catalogue of the Royal Artillery Museum indicates that he started negotiations to obtain 'our' bombard then. He was back in England by 1859 when he was Inspector-General of Army Schools and in 1860 became secretary to the important Ordnance Select Committee, responsible for the development and selection of weapons for the navy and army.

This was during the fundamental revolution in artillery materiel, from cast iron or bronze smooth-bore muzzle loaders, not greatly different from those of the sixteenth century, to wrought iron and steel rifled breech-loaders and rifled muzzle-loaders. Lefroy, not surprisingly, championed the new rifled guns but faced much opposition from traditionalist officers of the Royal Artillery. Being fortunate to work at Fort Nelson, one of the 'Palmerston forts', I am glad to note that Lefroy served on the Royal Commission of 1859. Reporting in 1860, it recommended a massive fort-building programme around Portsmouth, enthusiastically adopted by Lord Palmerston, if not so enthusiastically by his government colleagues.

After retiring from the army in 1870, Lefroy became a colonial governor, like many another Victorian soldier. His first posting was to Bermuda. Here he was known both for his attention to social welfare and for his scientific pursuits. He was so popular with the black population that he was known as 'the Negro Governor' by Bermuda's white racists. His extensive correspondence bears witness to his wide interests and knowledge, for example from Neolithic finds or runic inscriptions, to the early use of electricity for the North Foreland lighthouse. He received a knighthood in 1877.

Lefroy was well-known for his enormous capacity for hard work and for his learning. But he seems to have radiated charm - it is recorded that 'his clear blue eyes and winning smile invited confidence and admiration. Sir Henry was a devout member of the Anglican Church and a stalwart, kindly Christian gentleman.'[4] He seems to have been remarkably open-minded. Admiral Sir Henry Woods, who lived in Constantinople from 1867 until the early twentieth century, helping to run the Ottoman navy and serving as an ADC to Sultan Abdulhamid,

---

4 Ibid., 6.

provides another example of Victorian unconventionality:

> 'Never have I failed to be much impressed by the reverent attitude of the congregation and the solemnity of the service [at Hagia Sofia mosque] in striking contrast to what one sees sometimes in Western churches.[5]

Knowing of his interests it is not surprising to find that when in Turkey in 1855 Lefroy was on the lookout for prestigious additions to his cherished museum of artillery at the Rotunda, Woolwich. Close to the headquarters of the Royal Artillery and the vast Royal Arsenal, the Rotunda held an extraordinarily diverse collection, taking artillery in its old sense, it included all projectile weapons. But like some of the great continental collections, it included edged weapons and armour and thus to some extent duplicated the role of the Tower Armouries. There were trophies from numerous wars, gifts from foreign governments, archaeological finds and various curiosities. Near the Royal Military Academy, the museum, also known as the Royal Military Repository, served additionally as an important teaching collection. There was a special collection of heavy guns and mountings used for Repository Drill; this consisted of training gunners in heavy lifting and drill.

Even so, one might ask how Lefroy had come to place such importance on the heavy artillery of the Ottoman Turks. Doubtless he would have known of the considerable damage from such guns incurred by Sir John Duckworth's squadron forcing the Straits in 1807. But perhaps Lefroy's reading caught his imagination. He would surely have known Gibbon's *Decline and Fall of the Roman Empire*. In the last volume, Gibbon discusses Mehmet II's adoption of artillery and concludes that its battering of the walls of Constantinople was crucial to Mehmet's victory. So it seemed that for the first time, gunpowder artillery played part in one of the great events in world history. No artillerist of Lefroy's calibre could remain unmoved by Gibbon's lively appreciation of the young Mehmet's abilities:

> Among the instruments of destruction he studied with particular care the recent and tremendous discovery of the Latins, and his artillery surpassed whatever had yet appeared in the world. A

---

5   H. Woods, *Spunyarn from the Strands of a Sailor's Life Afloat and Ashore; Forty-seven Years under the Ensigns of Great Britain and Turkey* (London, 1924), 278.

Figure 4 Royal Armouries XIX.115 as illustrated by H. L. Blackmore

founder of cannon, a Dacian or Hungarian, who had been almost starved in the Greek service, deserted to the Muslims, and was liberally entertained by the Turkish Sultan. Mehmet was satisfied with the answer to his first question . . . 'Am I able to cast a cannon capable of throwing a ball or stone of sufficient size to batter the walls of Constantinople?' 'I am not ignorant of their strength; but were they more solid than the walls of Babylon, I could oppose an engine of superior power . . .'

Gibbon goes on to state, quoting Baron de Tott's memoirs:

A Turkish cannon, more enormous than that of Mehmet, still guards the entrance to the Dardanelles; and if the use be inconvenient, it has been found on late trial that the effect was far from contemptible... the ball traversed the Strait and leaving the waters in a foam... rose and bounded against the opposite hill.[6]

And if Lefroy could find no bombard definitely attributable to Mehmet's siege batteries of 1453, any early example would be an astounding addition to the collection at Woolwich. He made good contacts in the British diplomatic corps, obtaining from Mr W. H. Wrench, the Vice Consul at the Dardanelles, a list of all the early Turkish guns then existing in the forts on the Straits. Wrench included three that had been scrapped recently, one dated 1458 AD; two more were on the disposal list. Perhaps therefore, it did not seem too much to ask for one of these great bombards. Instead, Sultan Abdulmezit sent the fine early eighteenth-century culverin (figure 4).[7] It came straight to the Tower in 1857, complete with its carriage and sidearms. Perhaps it came to the Tower because it was not what Lefroy had hoped for. But Lefroy was not going to give up easily. In addition to persistence, though, he needed luck. Fortunately for him a state visit eventually seems to have created favourable conditions to solicit the gift.

---

6 E. Gibbon, *Decline and Fall of the Roman Empire* (London, 1887), vol. VIII, ch. LXVIII, 152.
7 Royal Armouries XIX.115. Blackmore (1976), catalogue no. 245.

Figure 5   Cartoon from 'Punch', 20 July 1867

THE ILLUSTRIOUS CONVALESCENT.

Mr. Bull.—"You a sick man! Ha! ha!—I knew my Crimean doctors would set you up, and this visit will do you all the good in the world."

. The Sultan of Turkey (Abdul Aziz) was at this time in London on a visit to the Queen. He was received everywhere with the greatest enthusiasm.

Constantinople was one of Britain's most important embassies. Sir Henry Bulwer, ambassador from 1858–65, maintained excellent contacts in Turkey and was on good terms with Sultan Abdulaziz (figure 5). Bulwer's opinions seem refreshingly independent. For example, writing to the Foreign Office, he considered that European influence and frequent censure of Turkey meant that, 'the energy natural to the [Turkish] race is paralyzed.'[8]

From Pera, he wrote to convey his assessment of the new Sultan: 'Economical in his expenses and not ostentatious or extravagant in his tastes. He still is fond of farming, shipping, horses, poetry – predilections which are all of a manly, useful and royal kind.'[9]

---

8   Letters from Bulwer to Lord John Russell, Foreign Minister 1859–65, The National Archives (TNA): FO 30/22, 17 April 1861.
9   Ibid., 26 June 1861.

Abdulaziz had frequent meetings with Bulwer which sound friendly and informal; the Sultan asked Bulwer if he should learn French. They discuss the Sultan's great desire to order ships to be built in Britain, including a yacht like Queen Victoria's for himself.[10] Such discussions produced great results for British shipbuilding. Three large ironclad warships were ordered from Robert Napier & Sons, Glasgow and were delivered in 1865. One, the *Abdul Aziz,* 'presents an unusually light and graceful appearance on the water' (figure 6). Launched at the end of 1864, she was 300 feet long and armed with sixteen 150-pounder Armstrong guns.

As well as strengthening the Ottoman forces, Sultan Abdulaziz intended to continue with the modernizing reforms begun by his predecessor Abdulmezit. He planned to make the first official visit to the West by any Sultan to see European progress for himself. He particularly wished to see the International Exhibition in Paris in 1867. The Sultan also hoped then to come to England, powerhouse of the industrial revolution and to meet Queen Victoria.[11]

Lord Lyons replaced Bulwer in 1865, serving until 1867. Lyons was not 'so sure about his [the Sultan's] visit to England'.[12] But the trip was quickly arranged for about 12 July backed by a formal invitation from

---

10 Ibid., 21 August 1861.
11 Letters from Bulwer to Lord Stanley, Foreign Minister 1866–68, TNA: FO 78/2010.
12 Ibid.

Queen Victoria, who generously offered the Sultan and his entourage the use of Buckingham Palace during their stay. Lyons wrote to Lord Stanley, on 10 June 1867:

> Our enemies suggest to the Sultan that a Constitutional Sovereign is very inferior to that of a Despot ... prove with every magnificence and show of public support that such is not the case in England.

And again on 12 June:

> It would be very desirable that we should confirm his impression that we are the first Naval Power and the richest Power. If we can give him a great naval Show ... we should do much to convince of our wealth as well as our strength on the sea.'[13]

The Foreign Office informed Lyons by telegram that, 'arrangements are made for a naval review on a large scale at Portsmouth'. As well as the Naval Review, visits to the Royal Arsenal, Woolwich, the Crystal Palace and the Tower were planned by the Lord Chamberlain office. The City of London was keen to offer a grand occasion at Guildhall (figure 7).

Lyons reported 'There will be nothing shocking to our notions or peculiar in the habits of the Sultan or his suite ...' There would be no women, no slaves, no eunuchs. The Sultan hoped 'to show the public in France and England how far the Turks have advanced in civilisation'.[14]

The visit seems to have gone well: it caused great excitement in London, with tremendous enthusiasm and rivalry for any chance of seeing the Sultan. *The Times* commented, 'The best Englishman this week is the man who enables the largest number of Englishwomen to see sights ... Turcomania is the order of the day.'[15]

Given the Sultan's visit to Woolwich, the use of the Royal Artillery for saluting and for escort duties, and Lefroy's eminence in the military establishment, it is safe to assume that he would have been present at one or more of the state occasions. He already knew Constantine Musurus Pasha, the Turkish ambassador to London, who was Greek and popular with Queen Victoria.

---

13 Letters from Lord Lyons to Lord Stanley, TNA: FO 78/2010, 10 and 12 June, 1867.
14 Ibid., 10 June 1867.
15 20 July 1867, 55.

Musurus was present when his Sultan received the Garter. This took place during the naval review, on board the Royal Yacht off Osborne House, Victoria's home on the Isle of Wight (figure 8). Here there might have been some shelter from the storm that raged that day. The brave *Times* reporter must have been on one of the very few spectator boats that ventured out, for he could see the scene unfold on the deck of the royal yacht, *Victoria & Albert*.

The queen recorded in her diary, 'I should have preferred the Star of India which is more suited for those who are not Christians'. But she noted, Abdulaziz 'had set his heart upon the garter'. In this, but not recorded by the queen, the Sultan was supported by the Prince of Wales – nothing less would do for an Emperor. Victoria was unaffected by the appalling weather, bemoaned at length in *The Times*, but she says the sea was very rough. The investiture gave Fuad Pasha, one of the sultan's chief ministers, the opportunity to reply for his master that the Queen had just made a Muslim monarch a Christian knight, and

Figure 7 Sultan welcomed at Guildhall (Illustrated London News, 27 July 1867, 88)

Figure 8   Sultan goes on board for Fleet Review, Clarence Yard, Gosport (Illustrated London News, 27 July 1867, 85)

EMBARKATION OF THE SULTAN AT CLARENCE-YARD, PORTSMOUTH, FOR THE NAVAL REVIEW.—SEE PAGE 87.

the Sultan, a Christian Bey a Muslim Pasha, since Abdulaziz had thus elevated Musurus.

The Sultan was welcomed back to Constantinople with extraordinary enthusiasm. Naval cooperation had been discussed during his visit, with the result that the Sultan's new navy was built in Britain, to become the third largest ironclad fleet in the world; in this and the merchant marine, many of the engineers and officers were British. British policy continued to support the Ottoman Empire as a counter to Russian influence in the Near East. This policy was hardly altruistic; it was intended to protect British India. It was a policy of enlightened self-interest: good for trade as well as security. British policy was thus to keep Turkey together. Turkey, the British ambassador was told by Czar Nicholas, was the 'sick man of Europe'. The Russians and the

French longed to break up the Ottoman empire and divide the spoils. Sir Henry Bulwer writing to the Foreign Office back in 1861 remarked, 'As usual I cannot give a flourishing account of our sick man . . . but he is living every day in spite of the very worst [symptoms]' and 'The conduct . . . of the majority of the Powers pledged to protect Turkey, is a disgrace . . .' He worries that France will try to split off Syria from Turkey. [16]

Reform was encouraged but later in his reign Abdulaziz became reclusive and failed to deal with the fundamental problems of the Turkish economy; perhaps the task was impossible, for the Ottoman Empire went bankrupt under his successor. But the Sultan had lost the confidence of his ministers. He was deposed and on 4 June 1876 apparently committed suicide, though it seems likely that he was in fact murdered.

But to return to the glory days around the Sultan's visit to Europe in 1867. The presentation of the great bombard must have been agreed during or soon after the Sultan's visit.

After the visit, Lefroy had continued his correspondence with Musurus, the ambassador to London, on artillery matters. The only clue as to the manner in which Lefroy finally obtained the bombard I have found is this. It is Musurus's reply to Lefroy in 1866 (figure 9).

I have received your kind letter of the 24th instant [July] relating to *ouvertures* made or about to be made by the British Government to the Sublime Porte in order to obtain one of the ancient guns of the Dardanelles.I will never forget the friendly and valuable assistance you rendered us last year, and it would give me great pleasure could I be useful to you in this instance. I think however that it is advisable to leave the matter entirely in the hand of the British Ambassador at Constantinople and to send the description of the gun to Lord Lyons either through the Foreign Office or privately . . . believe me, my dear general, yours very faithfully, C Musurus.[17]

Unfortunately Lefroy's copy letters on the subject do not exist, and were probably lost along with the Royal Artillery Institution file on the bombard when its archives were destroyed by bombing during

---

16 Letters from Bulwer to Lord John Russell, TNA: PRO 30/22, 17 April.
17 Archives of the Royal Artillery Museum, Woolwich.

Figure 9 The first page of Musurus's letter to General Lefroy

Figure 9 The first page of Musurus's letter to General Lefroy

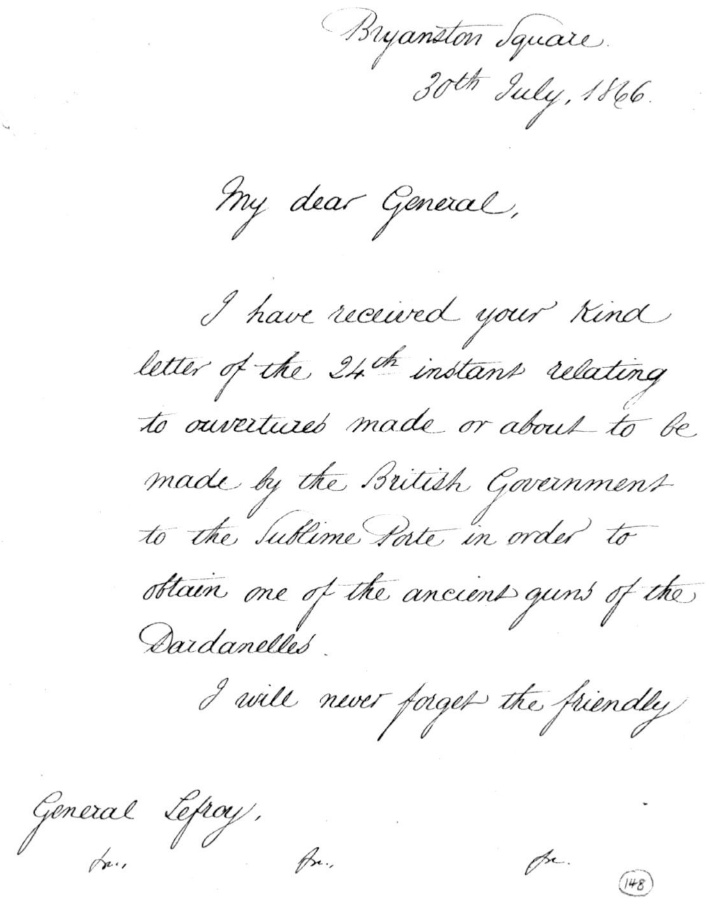

> Bryanston Square.
> 30th July, 1866.
>
> My dear General,
>
> I have received your kind letter of the 24th instant relating to ouvertures made or about to be made by the British Government to the Sublime Porte in order to obtain one of the ancient guns of the Dardanelles.
>
> I will never forget the friendly
>
> General Lefroy,
>
> (148)

the Second World War. However, if the presentation was not already agreed while the Sultan was in England, Lefroy's approach via the British embassy in Constantinople was no doubt favourably received during the period of Turkish euphoria following the Sultan's return after the state visit. In any dealings with the British Embassy in Constantinople, it might have helped that J. H. Wrench, with whom Lefroy had dealt back in 1855, was still there. Wrench became Consul and remained in Constantinople until his death in 1896, and was clearly an old 'Stamboul' hand.

But to whom the bombard was presented is not quite clear. Lefroy's paper, 'The Great Cannon of Muhammad II' was subtitled, 'recently presented to the British Government by the Sultan ...'[18] But in the text

18 Lefroy, 'The Great Cannon of Muhammad II', *Archaeological Journal* (1868), 261–80. This

he states, 'At the present time there are but 18 of these [early] guns left, including the one recently presented to Her Majesty . . . [i.e. Queen Victoria].'

The Woolwich Rotunda catalogue seems equally uncertain. In the introduction it says 'though Rotunda catalogues have always said it was presented . . . to Queen Victoria, this is not quite right. Lefroy . . . got it for the Rotunda in exchange for two Armstrong experimental pieces'. This was not generally known till he wrote his memoirs in 1895 and quoted the correspondence.[19] Then under its Rotunda inventory number, II.189, its provenance is given as 'presented to Her Majesty by Sultan Abdul Aziz, 1867'.[20] In fact, Lefroy died in 1890. I have not been able to consult a copy of his memoirs, published privately by his widow in 1895. Perhaps, in order to observe diplomatic niceties, the gift was, officially, from one sovereign to another, but that all along it was understood by officials that the bombard would go to Lefroy's beloved Rotunda.

The bombard was collected from the fort at Çanakkale by the Royal Navy using HMS *Terrible,* Captain Commerel CB, an old but large paddle-driven steamer. Operations commenced on 10 January 1868 in poor weather. It was decided to unscrew the barrel and chamber. Specially made capstan bars were used in the original recesses on the barrel and chamber, requiring a total force, applied by jacks, of 40 tons. Loading was completed on 18 January.[21] It arrived at Woolwich on 7 April 1868.

The great Turkish bombard remains a most evocative monument to medieval European technology and Turkish military innovation; it is a powerful reminder of the young Mehmet's apparently instinctive grasp of the possibilities of heavy artillery and his skill in deploying it.

---

very useful paper was also published by the Royal Artillery Institution.
19 Major P. Kaestlin, *Catalogue of the Museum of Artillery in the Rotunda at Woolwich. Part I, The Ordnance*, Manchester, 1963, rev. edn 1970, ix.
20 Ibid, 27.
21 Lefroy 1868, based on the log of HMS *Terrible.*

Diplomatic Gifts of Japanese Arms and Armour in the Nineteenth Century

Gregory Irvine
Victoria and Albert Museum

Although the active collecting of the Japanese sword in Britain did not begin until the second half of the nineteenth century, examples of swords and armour had found their way into the country from as early as the seventeenth century. In 1613 Captain John Saris, who had been running the trading post at Bantam in Java on behalf of the East India Company, was sent to Japan to establish a trading factory. He went with credentials from King James I (of England) and enlisted the help of Will Adams, an Englishman who had arrived in Japan in 1600 as the pilot of a Dutch trading vessel and who had risen to become the Shōgun Tokugawa Ieyasu's chief advisor on foreign affairs.

Saris did not stay in Japan for very long and endured many frustrations before leaving in December 1613. He did, however, return bearing gifts from the shōgun Tokugawa Ietada for King James. In the record of his brief stay in Japan Saris makes several references to receiving gifts of swords which he refers to as 'cattan' (katana) for himself.[1] He also describes gifts of 'two Pikes or Iapan staves with Cattans or Sables [sabres] on the ends' – presumably some form of naginata. The armours are to be found in the Royal Armouries collection, but of the 'cattan'

---

1   Sir Ernest M. Satow (ed.), *The Voyage of Captain John Saris to Japan, 1613* (London, 1900), 101: 'After midnight the ould King sent to the howse, to intreat me to send Mr. Cocks and my linguist to him, which I did. The occatyon was to intreat me to excuse him for that he came not so offten to vizite me as formerly; the reason was for that he douted a spie to be in Towne, sent by the Emperor to take notis what curtesyes past betwene us; notwithstanding he would not want now and then to come vnto me, expecting the like from me; And sent unto me by him a Cattan, which for manye yeares he had worne himselfe, intreating me to accept thereof, and keepe it for his sake.'

Figure 1   Presented by the Earl of Fife, April 23rd 1813: 'A curious old sword of one of the Moorish Kings of Spain' in the Royal Collection inventory of the North Corridor, no. 1659; only the photograph survives (V&A)

and 'Iapan staves with cattans on the ends' we have no record. He was also censured by the Court of the East India Company for bringing back 'certain lascivious books and pictures' – which were ordered to be removed and burned . . . [2]

It is not until after the so-called 're-opening' of Japan (following Commodore Perry's arrival in 1853) that the active collecting of Japanese swords in Britain began, although there are some poorly documented examples of swords before this time. For example, in the Royal Collection, Windsor Castle (listed in the pre-1860 North Corridor Inventory, no. 1659) there is a Japanese sword 'Presented by the Earl of Fife, April 23rd 1813' and described as 'A curious old sword of one of the Moorish Kings of Spain' (figure 1). This perhaps reminds us that the Japanese armour given to James I was once described as an armour of the 'Great Moghul'.

---

2   Ibid., lxvii.

Figure 2   Top, the original Japanese list of diplomatic gifts (TNA: FO46/8/107) and below, translation of the Japanese documents (TNA: FO46/8 p. 102, July 14 1859 and FO46/8 p.347, March 21 1860)

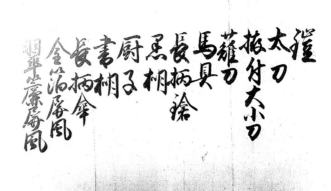

Soon after the establishment of an official British presence in Japan there was an exchange of diplomatic gifts between Tokugawa Iemochi, the last but one of the Tokugawa shōguns, and Queen Victoria through the offices of Sir Rutherford Alcock, who was appointed Britain's first Consul General in Japan, in 1859.

In an official despatch of 14 July 14 1859, Alcock wrote to Lord John Russell, British Foreign Secretary:

> The day after the ratifications [of the Treaty of Edo] were exchanged I received intimation from the Tycoon[3] that His Majesty had caused a list of articles to be prepared as a present to the Queen which he desired might be received and forwarded.[4]

The gift was, however, not immediately forthcoming and the Japanese prevaricated, using various delaying tactics including the disruption caused by a major fire at Edo Castle in 1860; Alcock considered this to be yet another convenient excuse for the Japanese authorities not to implement a number of other important decisions. Alcock was informed that many of the gifts had been destroyed in the fire and it was not until 1 September that he could write in a private letter that

> I believe the Queen's presents are really to be ready shortly. I had begun to doubt whether they had not dropped them for they [the Japanese] are not liberally disposed.

Finally, on 15 December 1860, Alcock wrote to Lord Russell that the gift had at last been received and was being crated and shipped to Britain via Shanghai on the steamship *England*.[5]

The 1859 translation of the Japanese list is reasonably accurate, but the list of 1860 appears to suggest that the contents of the gift have changed. For example the '*yoloi*' has apparently been replaced by 'a mail coat and helmet', though this may simply be a confused western terminology.[6]

---

3 The shōgun; there was much confusion on the part of westerners as to who actually ruled Japan. Emperor Kōmei retained only symbolic power at his court in Kyoto.

4 The National Archives (TNA): FO 46/3 pp. 102–7.

5 R. Fortune, *Yedo and Peking: a Narrative to the Capitals of Japan and China* (London, 1863), 151.

6 TNA: FO 46/8 pp. 345–7.

Figure 3   Suit of armour in Ō-yoroi style (V&A 362–1865)

In 1865 the South Kensington Museum (as the V&A was then called) received a substantial gift of Japanese objects from Queen Victoria. It has always been assumed that this was the 1860 diplomatic gift but what was received at the museum was substantially different from either of Alcock's lists. We may speculate whether there may have been subsequent diplomatic gifts which could have been amalgamated

Figure 4   Katana by Ishidō Korekazu (V&A 263–1865)

with the original gift before the donation to the V&A, or indeed that the queen was simply passing on items from the gift together with other Japanese objects in her collection. 'Missing' items, such as the screens, could be explained by the Royal Collection retaining items (and indeed, the Royal Collection at Windsor may still have objects believed to be from this original gift), but the numerous additional objects pose further questions.

The South Kensington Museum received no 'mail coat and helmet', but did in fact receive a splendid Ō-yoroi – Rutherford's 'Yoloï' (figure 3). Nor did it receive fifty 'Nagaze Yali', but only ten spears. Furthermore the museum received considerable amounts of lacquer, porcelain, textiles, two complete sets of horse trappings and only two

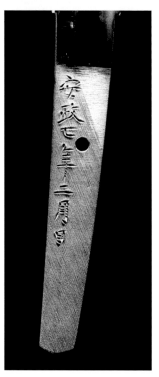

*Figure 5   Katana
by Ishidō Korekazu
Seitan saku (V&A
266–1865)*

screens (from the original listing of some thirty-six screens). Museum documentation is patchy but the printed lists relating to the gift describe most of the gift as being 'modern'. [7]

The Japanese arms and armour which the museum received were as follows:

> 248 to 257-1865: 10 spears (248 and 249 'Transferred to Museum Edinburgh')
> 259 to 266-1865: 9 swords (259 and 264 'Transferred to Museum, Edinburgh')
> 267 to 271-1865: 5 sword sheaths (269 'Transferred to Museum, Edinburgh')
> 362-1865: suit of armour
> 363 and 364-1865: two sets of horse-trappings

---

7   Inventory of Objects Acquired in the Year 1865, pp. 4–65. V&A bound volume 'Circulation: Inventory of Objects in the South Kensington Museum II, 1860–1867'.

These examples of Japanese arms and armour were the first to enter the museum's collections and the swords carry inscriptions which indicate that they were made especially for this diplomatic gift. It is probable that the swords from the 1859 list were destroyed in the Edo castle fire and then hurriedly replaced by new blades in 1860.

The O-yoroi is a superb example of a late Edo period copy of an armour of the Kamakura period (1185–1333), but with embellishments that would not be found on original armour of that period – for example the haidate is a later device, possibly originating around the end of the thirteenth century. It does, however, represent the type of ceremonial armour and military equipment that were being produced under the nationalistic revival of the early nineteenth century. This 'revival' was perhaps not entirely coincidental as the ruling samurai classes had by this time become little more than administrators along with the demise of the martial spirit of 'Old Japan', so a harking back to the 'glorious' past was almost inevitable.

The helmet is signed 'Myochin Mondo Ki no Muneharu, on a day in the eight month of the sixth [*tsuchinoto hitsuji*] year of Ansei' (equivalent to 1859). Again, can we speculate that this was in fact made for the 'original' gift? The Myochin family had a long tradition (documented back to the sixteenth century) of producing armour for Japan's ruling military class so it is most likely that the armour was at the least assembled specifically for the diplomatic gift.

Curiously the gift included several empty *shirasaya*, the type of scabbard used to house a sword without mounts. They are described in the museum's records as 'sword sheath, white wood, quite plain, in process of manufacture, the lacquer not yet having been applied'. Also included were four sake flasks (figure 6), one still containing sake – we do not know what happened to the contents of the other three . . . The 'full' bottle was opened some years ago by the late Dr Oliver Impey who pronounced it to be not especially good, but having a heavenly scent . . .

Although Alcock was not recalled from Japan until 1864, he had personally accumulated enough Japanese objects to be sent to the London International Exhibition of 1862 (figure 7). The *Catalogue of Works of Industry and Art sent from Japan by Rutherford Alcock Esq., C.B. Her Majesty's Envoy Extraordinary and Minister Plenipotentiary at*

*Figure 6   Sake flask
(V&A 311–1865)*

*Figure 7   The
Japan section of the
London International
Exhibition of 1862
(Illustrated London
News, 20 September
1862)*

the Court of the Tycoon has over 600 entries relating to Japan. Alcock's
introduction to the catalogue for the exhibition refers to the types of
objects exhibited:

... others are very costly, and only to be obtained at prices, which in Europe would probably be thought far disproportioned to their value; but these are chiefly specimens of ... swords and armour, of which latter class the armed retainers of the Daimios, and feudal chiefs themselves, are extravagant admirers; and when wealthy, they will give any price for an approved weapon by a maker of great repute.[8]

The exhibition of objects assembled by Alcock included catalogue number 491, 'Japanese long two-handed sword', and number 492, 'Short sword of one of the party of assassins which attacked the British Legation on 5th July, 1861.' Japan was still in huge turmoil as the samurai class tried to hang on to power in the face of a large group who thought (with justification) that their time was past and that Japan should modernize (for this read 'westernize'). Westerners, having arrived in large numbers from 1853 were very much seen as intruders and ran the risk of almost daily attack.

Alcock's successor in Japan, Sir Harry Parkes took up office in 1865 as 'Her Majesty's Envoy Extraordinary and Minister Plenipotentiary and Consul-General in Japan' and during this time he was present at the overthrow of the shōgunal system of government and the emperor's restoration to power in January 1868.

Resentment against foreigners continued unabated and on 23rd March 1868 Parkes and his entourage were attacked while on their way to an audience with the newly reappointed emperor in Kyoto. Parkes set out with his translators Algernon Bertram Freeman-Mitford and Ernest Mason Satow and an escort of British cavalry and Japanese troops. Two Japanese fanatics armed with long swords attacked the entourage at a narrow crossroads which prevented the use of the cavalry lances and they caused considerable casualties before one was killed and the other incapacitated. The imperial audience was eventually held on 26 March 1868, and Parkes finally presented his credentials to the Emperor Meiji as the first fully accredited British minister to Japan.

Mitford gave a graphic description of the attack in a letter to *The Times* of 20 May 1868. He also gave details of the part played by the Japanese members of the group, particularly Nakai Kōzō, 'a Japanese

---

8 *Catalogue of Works of Industry and Art . . .* (London, 1862), 2.

Figure 8   English army officer's curved Mameluk pattern levée sword (Kyoto National Museum)

officer of rank, formerly of the Satsuma clan' and Gotō Kōjirō 'a high officer of the Foreign Department'. Nakai tried to cut down the attackers but stumbled on his long trousers and was himself cut. Gotō came to his rescue and between the two of them killed and decapitated one of the attackers. The other, despite having been cut, bayoneted, lanced and shot in the head, survived and on interrogation was discovered to be a renegade priest with no motives other than to kill any foreigners he met.[9]

On a visit to the Kyoto National Museum the curator Mr Kubo showed me a box and some documents and asked me if they were of any interest. I was astonished to find the original faded letters from Parkes to Nakai thanking him for his (and Gotō's) efforts in defending the British party. There is also one of two presentation swords still in its original box (figure 8). This is one of the '. . . swords of honour presented to both Nakai and Gotō, in token of her appreciation of their gallantry

---

9 G. Irvine 'Sensation Diplomacy. Sir Harry Parkes and Japan: 1865–1871', *Royal Armouries Yearbook*, 2 (1997), 156–60.

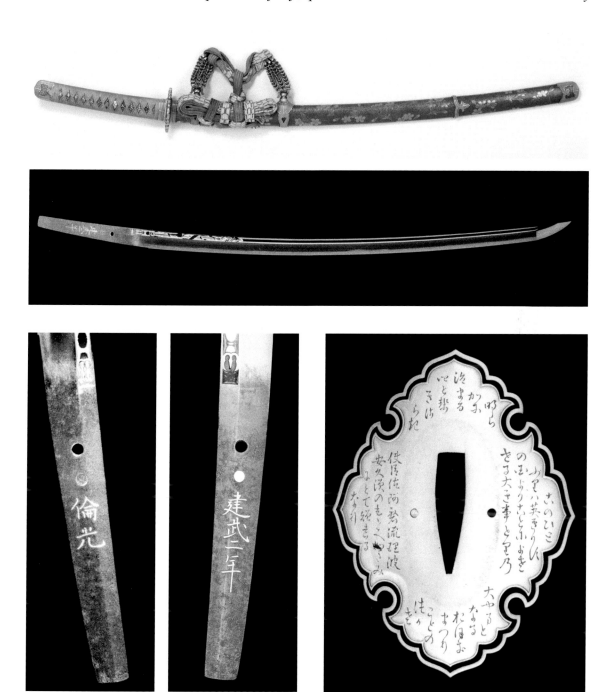

Figure 9   Ito-maki-no tachi mounting with metal fittings (including the suspension chains) of solid gold by Ota Yoshihisa and the Ō-zeppa (V&A M.13-1949)

on this occasion' from Queen Victoria. The sword is modelled on the English army officer's curved Mameluk pattern levée sword by Charles Smith and Co. of 5 New Burlington Street, London. Quite what the Japanese made of this, to their eyes, perhaps rather bizarre sword has not been recorded.

Parkes had never been noted for his patience and in his dealings with the procrastinating Japanese officials he often threatened and bullied them in a fashion which would never have been acceptable in western diplomatic circles. Nevertheless, he gained great respect from the Japanese and before he briefly left Japan in 1871 for a rest of almost two years, he was afforded the singular honour of a private audience with the Emperor Meiji in May of that year and was presented with a superb sword. Parkes remained in post until 1883 but when he finally returned to England, the sword was given to the South Kensington Museum in 1873 where it was recorded in the museum archives as 'A Sword of State presented to him by the Mikado of Japan'. [10]

The sword has the inlaid gold signature of the smith Tomomitsu and the date of Kemmu 2 (1335). A professional appraiser has inscribed the name of Tomomitsu (of Osafune in Bizen Province) and the year of manufacture in gold on the tang. This was a period in Japan's history know as the Nanbokucho (northern and southern courts) when there were two claimants to the imperial throne. The Kemmu period falls within the reign of Emperor Go-Daigo of the Southern Court. The graceful blade, with the long curved point (*kissaki*) so typical of the Nanbokucho period, has been considerably shortened and any original signature would have been lost in this process.

The Ō-zeppa, a plate on the tsuba (sword-guard) has a dedicatory inscription which indicates that the blade was re-mounted with new fittings and assembled especially for Parkes, most likely on the orders of the emperor himself.

The understanding of the Japanese sword in the West was, at this time, virtually non-existent and much dubious information on the subject offered by the Japanese themselves was taken at face value. Many swords which started to appear were outright fakes or thought to be of great antiquity. Although not a diplomatic gift, in 1888 in the first acquisition of a Japanese sword since the gift from Queen Victoria,

---

10 V&A Nominal File 'Parkes, Sir H', MA/1/P356.

the South Kensington Museum was offered a 'Fine old carved ivory Japanese Royal State Sword, (early 18th century) for sale at £95'. This would be equivalent to about £7,000 today (figure 10).

The museum accepted the sword on the grounds that 'This is so important an example of Japanese Art both in design and the execution of the ivory carving that it is most desirable for the museum collection. The price asked is very reasonable.' The ivory scabbard obviously dates from about 1870 and the sword blade is actually signed Kubota Minamoto Muneaki (a well-documented swordsmith) and dated equivalent to 1857.

The museum continued to benefit from diplomatic gifts, with excellent Japanese swords being donated by the widow of Sir Claude MacDonald (1852–1915), British ambassador to Japan from 1905 to 1912. MacDonald was appointed Consul-General for the Empire of Japan in October 1900 and became Britain's first ambassador to Japan when the status of the legation was raised to an embassy in 1905.

His widow, Lady Ethel left several superb swords (with excellent mounts) on loan to the V&A in 1915; in 1929 she changed the loan to a permanent gift.[11] The V&A file contains some fascinating documentation relating to MacDonald's interest in Japanese swords – including a personally annotated (undated) Japanese sale catalogue of Japanese swords.

Perhaps the most splendid of the swords is a fourteenth-century blade by Morimitsu in a superb *ito-maki-no-tachi* mounting (figure 11). According to a letter from Lady Ethel this sword was given to Sir Claude by Prince Katsura Taro (1848–1913), a general in the Imperial Japanese Army and three times prime minister of Japan.

Figure 10   Tachi in ivory mounts, blade signed Kubota Minamoto (V&A 1708-188)

---

11   V&A Nominal File MacDonald, Lady Ethel. MA/1//M53

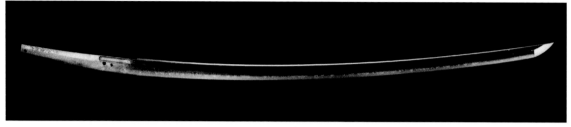

Figure 11   Ito–maki-no tachi mount and Tachi blade signed Morimitsu of Osafune in Bizen (V&A M.139-1929)

Another sword from this gift bears an inscription which indicates that the blade was made literally in front of MacDonald by Sugawara Kanenori, one of the Emperor Meiji's *Teishistu Gigei'in*, imperial craftsmen (figure 12).

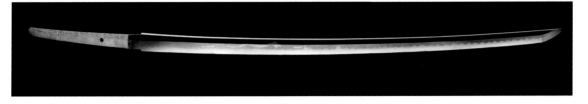

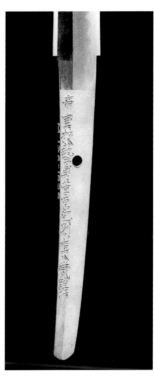

Figure 12   Tachi blade by Sugawara Kanenori (V&A M.136-1929)

There have since been very few diplomatic gifts of Japanese arms and armour though two swords dated 1922 were donated to the V&A by Edward, Prince of Wales (later Edward VIII, then Duke of Windsor) having received them on his visit to Japan that year.

The final diplomatic gift, although here diplomacy in a different form, came from Major (later Colonel) John Arthur Coghill Somerville (1872–1955) who was military attaché at the British Embassy in Tokyo between 1911 and 1914 and served under MacDonald (figure 13). Speculating again, we might think of these two military men spending time in Tokyo discussing the merits and beauty of the Japanese sword.

Figure 13   Katana blade by Tsunahiro of Soshū + shirasaya with ink inscriptions (V&A M.356-1940)

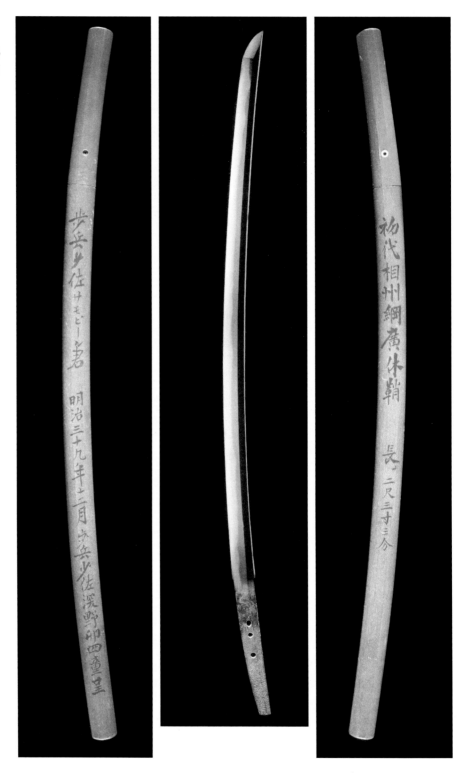